Elite • 172

Roman Battle Tactics
390–110 BC

NIC FIELDS ILLUSTRATED BY GERRY & SAM EMBLETON

Consultant editor Martin Windrow

First published in Great Britain in 2010 by Osprey Publishing,
Midland House, West Way, Botley, Oxford OX2 0PH, UK
44-02 23rd St, Suite 219, Long Island City, NY 11101, USA
Email: info@ospreypublishing.com

Print ISBN: 978 1 84603 382 7
ebook ISBN: 978 1 84908 124 5

Editor: Martin Windrow
Design: Ken Vail Graphic Design, Cambridge, UK (kvgd.com)
Typeset in Sabon and Myriad Pro
Index by Fineline Editorial Services
Originated by PPS Grasmere, Leeds, UK
Printed in China through World Print Ltd.

10 11 12 13 14   10 9 8 7 6 5 4 3 2 1

A CIP catalogue record for this book is available from the British Library

ARTIST'S NOTE

Readers may care to note that the original paintings from which the
colour plates in this book were prepared are available for private sale.
All reproduction copyright whatsoever is retained by the Publishers.
All enquiries should be addressed to:

www.gerryembleton.com

The Publishers regret that they can enter into no correspondence upon
this matter.

THE WOODLAND TRUST

Osprey Publishing are supporting the Woodland Trust, the UK's leading
woodland conservation charity, by funding the dedication of trees.

GLOSSARY

Singular, plural:

Acies	line-of-battle
Ala, alae	'wing' – Latin/Italian unit comparable to *legio* (q.v.)
As, asses	small copper coin, worth $\frac{1}{10}$ of *denarius*
Centurio, centuriones	officer in command of *centuria* (q.v.)
Centuria, centuriae	administrative sub-unit of *manipulus* (q.v.)
Decurio, decuriones	officer in command of *turma* (q.v.)
Imperium	coercive power of higher magistrates
La Tène	Iron Age culture named after site at La Tène, Lac de Neuchâtel
Legio, legiones	'levy' – principal unit of Roman army
Manipulus, manipuli	'handful' – tactical sub-unit of *legio* (q.v.)
Optio, optiones	second-in-command of *centuria/turma* (q.v.)
Praetorium	consul's headquarters tent
Tribunus, tribuni	'tribal leader' – military tribune
Turma, turmae	tactical sub-unit of cavalry
Villanovan	Iron Age culture named after a site at Villanova, near Bologna

FOR A CATALOGUE OF ALL BOOKS PUBLISHED BY OSPREY MILITARY
AND AVIATION PLEASE CONTACT:

Osprey Direct, c/o Random House Distribution Center,
400 Hahn Road, Westminster, MD 21157
Email: uscustomerservice@ospreypublishing.com

Osprey Direct, The Book Service Ltd, Distribution Centre,
Colchester Road, Frating Green, Colchester, Essex, CO7 7DW
E-mail: customerservice@ospreypublishing.com

www.ospreypublishing.com

CONTENTS

ROMAN BATTLE TACTICS 390–146 BC

In Roman legend Rhea Silvia, mother of Romulus and Remus, was a Vestal Virgin who claimed that Mars, god of war, was the father of the twins. This tradition expresses how the Romans chose to view and represent themselves, as divinely gifted with overwhelming superiority in warfare. (Ludovisi, Mars Ultor; Rome, MNR Palazzo Altemps, 8654; photo Fields-Carré Collection)

INTRODUCTION

The history of Roman battle tactics is a story of two extreme models of army organization and deployment. When Rome was a hilltop village on the Tiber, its wars were little more than sudden smash-and-grab raids; the first model, therefore, is of armies that are little more than warrior bands. By the time that Rome was a city pursuing regional dominance, Roman warfare had become an adaptation of Greek hoplite warfare, based on the ideology of the decisive pitched battle; and when Rome had grown into the competitive, plundering power that confronted Hannibal, the army had assumed the more familiar form of the manipular legion. In both these latter cases the model is that of the disciplined infantry formation in a set-piece battle – first the rigid phalanx, and then the more flexible legion, but both with an excellence in and a preference for the head-to-head battle that destroys the enemy.

It is certainly true that Rome's soldiers (and those of its Italian allies, the *socii*) were essentially a militia, called up to serve in one of the legions for a few weeks over the summer and then dismissed to their everyday occupations. We must assume that in periods of prolonged campaigning many gained considerable experience of soldiering, but few, if any, were professional soldiers in the sense that they knew no other life. Yet we should not underestimate the fighting qualities of the provisional manipular legion, since this was the weapon with which Rome would win its place as the chief city of the Mediterranean world.

Along the path that was to lead from obscurity to dominance of its world, Rome's part-time citizen soldiery were to suffer a series of catastrophic defeats. The successive military disasters at Lake Trasimene and Cannae in 217–216 BC would cost the Romans 15,000 and

50,000 men respectively, each in a single day. The butcher's bill at Cannae – horrendous in both absolute and relative terms, i.e. as a percentage of the force deployed – may not have been equalled in Europe until World War I. It could be argued that the inexperience of Roman soldiers and the rigidity of Roman tactics were responsible for such casualty rates, but they should not blind us to the fact that over the longer term the manipular legion performed remarkably well in the quick, decisive, head-on clash with the enemy. As Polybios rightly points out, 'the defeats they suffered had nothing to do with weapons or formations, but were brought about by Hannibal's cleverness and military genius' (18.28.7). In this Rome was disadvantaged by the limited ability of its aristocratic generals, but there is no real proof that the employment of grim professional soldiers in command would have improved matters. Hannibal's obvious skill as a general inflicted these catastrophic defeats on this militia army; yet Rome's powers of resilience were so impressive that the same type of army, when better led and with higher morale, beat him in turn at Zama in 202 BC.

The Roman military system was precisely that – a system. Rome did not need brilliant generals, and rarely produced them; it just needed to replicate its legions, which it did on an almost industrial basis. The inclusion of Italian allies within the army of this period did not change its essential tactical doctrines, since most allied units – the *alae* of Roman armies – were probably disciplined, organized and equipped like the legions, and thus fought in a similar way. By an ironic but saving paradox, Romans were at their very best only when in the direst circumstances: in times of even the most serious setbacks they could take the long view, because Rome never gave up. If the

Rome's founding by Romulus is traditionally dated at 753 BC. Abandoned at birth, he and his twin Remus – whom he later fought and killed – were believed to have been abandoned after birth, but suckled by a she-wolf, and later raised by the wife of a shepherd. The myth is in fact much later than the 8th century BC, but the date itself is plausible. This Etruscan sculpture, known as the *Lupa Capitolina*, had the suckling twins added in the 15th century AD. (Fields-Carré Collection)

real secret of Rome's success was the ability to withstand appalling losses and the willingness of its ordinary citizens (and *socii*) to persist in warfare year after year, then we should also remember that all this carnage was accomplished at close range, mostly in the fierce but carefully drilled hand-to-hand combat at which Roman soldiers excelled.

The combination of superior organization and training and the high lethality of their small arms – both unmatched for many centuries following their age – goes a long way towards explaining the very high numbers of battle casualties suffered by ancient armies when compared with those of the medieval and early modern centuries. In almost all respects, the conduct of war would not return to the levels of sophistication and effectiveness demonstrated by the Romans until at least the 17th century AD. Tactics as a practical art remained in decline for more than a thousand years after Rome's extinction, and it may even be argued that general standards of tactical flexibility remained inferior to those of Roman armies until the era of Napoleon. Moreover, the destructiveness of war had reached a very advanced state long before the introduction of modern weapons of mass destruction. The removal of Carthage from the map in 146 BC may have taken longer to accomplish than that of Hiroshima in 1945, but the level of destruction was just as complete and merciless. No other army before the modern epoch would attain the sheer efficiency of the Roman legionary army, which was not a purely military institution like that of a modern state. The middle Republic was a society superbly organized for war, and its army was a microcosm of that society. Its capacity for sustained, long-range, aggressive war-making had no earlier parallel, and was to have none again until the rise of modern European nation states.

CHRONOLOGY OF MAJOR CONFLICTS

753 BC	Traditional date for the foundation of Rome by Romulus
509 BC	Traditional date for expulsion of Rome's last king, Tarquinius Superbus
496 BC	Latin League defeated at Lake Regillus

4th century BC:

396 BC	Fall of Veii
390 BC	Romans defeated at Allia; Gauls sack Rome (387 BC, according to Polybios)
343–341 BC	First Samnite War (doubted by some scholars)
340–338 BC	Latin War
326–304 BC	Second Samnite War
321 BC	Romans defeated at Caudine Forks

3rd century BC:

298–290 BC	Third Samnite War
295 BC	Romans defeat Samnites and Gauls at Sentinum
280–275 BC	War against Pyrrhos of Epeiros
280 BC	Romans defeated at Herakleia
279 BC	Romans defeated at Asculum
275 BC	Pyrrhos defeated at Malventum (Beneventum)
272 BC	Fall of Taras (Tarentum)
264–241 BC	First Punic War

BELOW LEFT
This southern Italian 'muscle cuirass' has been dated to the second half of the 4th century BC; the lack of shoulder-guards distinguishes such armours from Greek examples. (British Museum; photo N.V. Sekunda)

BELOW
Another common type of cuirass among the Samnites and other Oscan peoples was this pair of almost square bronze plates; the crude decoration in imitation of the human torso immediately recalls the more finished Greek-style muscle cuirass seen in Etruscan sculptures. This find is southern Italian, c. 375–325 BC. (British Museum: photo N.V. Sekunda)

260 BC	Roman naval victory off Mylae
256 BC	Roman naval victory off Ecnomus
255 BC	Defeat of Regulus in Africa
249 BC	Roman naval defeat off Drepana
241 BC	Roman naval victory off Aegates Islands
240–237 BC	Mercenary War in Africa
238 BC	Rome annexes Sardinia
229–228 BC	First Illyrian War
225 BC	Gauls defeated at Telamon
222 BC	Insubres defeated at Clastidium and Mediolanum
219 BC	Second Illyrian War; Hannibal captures Saguntum
218–201 BC	Second Punic War
218 BC	Romans defeated at Ticinus and Trebbia
217 BC	Romans defeated at Lake Trasimene
216 BC	Romans defeated at Cannae; Capua revolts

The Arnoaldi *situla,* a bronze bucket of *c.* 450 BC, depicts chariots and warriors on foot in some detail. The latter carry the Italic body shield or *scutum;* this had only a single, horizontal handgrip in the centre, protected by a large wooden spine with a metal boss plate. This allowed it to be moved about freely in combat, and the boss could be used to punch an adversary. (Bologna, Museo Civico Archeologico; Ancient Art & Architecture)

215 BC	Alliance of Carthage with Philip V of Macedon and Syracuse
214–205 BC	First Macedonian War
213 BC	Hannibal occupies Tarentum; Romans besiege Syracuse
212 BC	Romans besiege Capua
211 BC	Hannibal marches on Rome; fall of Capua and Syracuse
209 BC	Recapture of Tarentum; Scipio takes New Carthage
207 BC	Hasdrubal Barca defeated at Metaurus
206 BC	Scipio's victory at Ilipa
203 BC	Scipio's victory at Great Plains
202 BC	Scipio's victory at Zama
200–197 BC	Second Macedonian War

2nd century BC:

197 BC	Philip V of Macedon defeated at Kynoskephalai
194 BC	Romans evacuate Greece
192–189 BC	War against Antiochos III of Syria
191 BC	Antiochos defeated at Thermopylai
190 BC	Antiochos defeated at Magnesia
189 BC	Romans plunder Galatia
181–179 BC	First Celtiberian War
172–168 BC	Third Macedonian War
168 BC	Perseus of Macedon defeated at Pydna
154–138 BC	Lusitanian War
153–151 BC	Second Celtiberian War
149–148 BC	Fourth Macedonian War
149–146 BC	Third Punic War
147–146 BC	Achaean War
146 BC	Sack of Corinth; destruction of Carthage

ITALY BEFORE ROME

As with most regions in the Mediterranean basin, the country now known as Italy is divided into barren mountains lacking good soils, and low-lying, fertile coastal regions – a topography that encouraged regional separatism. Around the beginning of the Italic Iron Age (*c.* 1000 BC) a number of regional populations can be identified and given distinct ethnic labels. They can be differentiated partly by their language, and partly by distinctive customs such as the use of characteristic artefacts, burial practices and religious cults.

THE ETRUSCANS

Etruria broadly corresponds to Tuscany, a volcanic and fertile land between the Arno and Tiber rivers, from the Apennines to the Tyrrhenian Sea. The enigmatic people we know as the Etruscans (Etrusci), the original creators of Italy, were probably not Indo-European in origin. Although we have many of their texts, their language – which can be deciphered, since it uses the Greek alphabet – has yet to be fully understood. What is clear is that their material culture developed out of the Villanovan culture of northern and central Italy as a result of increasing contact with the Greeks.

The Etruscan heyday was in the 6th century BC, when they expanded at the expense of the Italic peoples, north across the Apennine watershed and into the Po valley, and south into Campania, where the Greeks had arrived before them. The

4th-century BC bronze statuette of a Samnite warrior. He wears an Attic helmet (with holes that once held feathers), a characteristic triple-disc cuirass, a broad Oscan belt and Graeco-Etruscan greaves. His shield and spear are missing. After a series of hard wars Rome eventually absorbed this people and converted them into allies who supplied troops to fight in its wars. (Paris, Musée du Louvre, Br 124; photo Fields-Carré Collection)

political structure that underpinned this expansion remains a mystery; at this time the Etruscans seem to have been organized into a loose confederation of largely autonomous cities, but whether or not such a socio-political pattern was sufficient to support such distant conquests remains debatable. One of the settlements that passed under Etruscan control was Rome, where an Etruscan dynasty was installed in the closing years of the 7th century BC. The site was the last point before the sea where the Tiber could conveniently be crossed, thus giving the Etruscans access to Latium and southwards into Campania. Among its other attractions the most important was salt, an essential commodity: the salt-road (called by the Romans the Via Salaria) led from the only salt-beds in western Italy, which lay on the north bank of the Tiber's mouth, past Rome and so up the Tiber to Etruscan cities such as Clusium and Perusia.

A village called Rome

Far enough from the sea to protect its first inhabitants from the danger of piracy, the site of Rome lay some 20km (12 miles) upstream on the east bank of the river Tiber, at its lowest crossing point before its mouth on the Tyrrhenian Sea. This convenient ford, which lay below an island in the river, was overlooked by a group of hills. Watered by an adequate number of springs, well wooded, fairly precipitous and defensible, these hills provided early settlers with refuge from flooding and some protection against predators. Despite the boasts of Augustan historians, in the early days nothing seemed to single out this modest riverine settlement for future greatness. In these obscure times Rome was allied with other Latin settlements in Latium, and the seasonal battles that preoccupied these Italic people were little more than squabbles over cattle herds, water rights and arable land.

Tradition dates the foundation of Rome to the year 753 BC, and archaeology tells us that in the beginning there were two distinct settlements, one on the Palatine hill and one on the Esquiline. The Palatine was the supposed site of Romulus' foundation, and there is clear evidence of Iron Age dwellings of posts, wattle and daub, and of pit burials (*a pozza* cremations), at the time of the traditional foundation and even earlier. There is also archaeological evidence for Iron Age settlement on the Esquiline; but although the inhabitants of these hilltop villages shared a common culture, finds from the latter site have their parallels in southern Latium, while those from the Palatine are closer in typology to the Villanovans of the Alban hills. Moreover, the Esquiline trench burials (*a fossa* inhumations) of the beginning of the 7th century BC contain grave goods that suggest to some scholars an intrusion of the Sabines. It seems likely that these easily defended hills, rising at a convenient crossing of the Tiber and with good pasture, attracted two separate bands of semi-nomadic herdsmen down from the Alban and Sabine mountains. There may therefore be some substance to the legend, as retold by Livy, of the foundation from Alba Longa (1.3.4) and of the fusion between the Romans and the Sabines (1.13). So Rome began as clusters of huts forming independent hamlets, which coalesced only gradually and perhaps painfully into a unified village settlement.

THE LATINS

The Latins (Latini) gave their name to Latium, the open country south of the lower reaches of the Tiber. This is the ethno-cultural group to which the Romans mainly belonged. In the early Iron Age this people consisted of a group of communities – traditionally given as 30 – who spoke the Latin language, and gathered each year to celebrate the festival of Jupiter Latiaris on the Alban Mountain. Archaeology has demonstrated that they also had some distinctive artefacts and burial practices. By the 7th century BC at the latest these communities were grouped into a confederation for purposes of religion, and by the following century this confederation had taken on the form of a political and military league.

THE OSCANS

In the central section of the Apennine chain that forms the spine of the Italian peninsula, most of the Italic peoples spoke a language called Oscan, a tongue closely related to Latin but with some distinctive characteristics. The Oscan-speakers were divided into various groupings, the most important of which were the Samnites who inhabited the mountainous region due east of Rome, down to the area behind Campania. At the time of their long, hard wars with the Romans the Samnites consisted of four

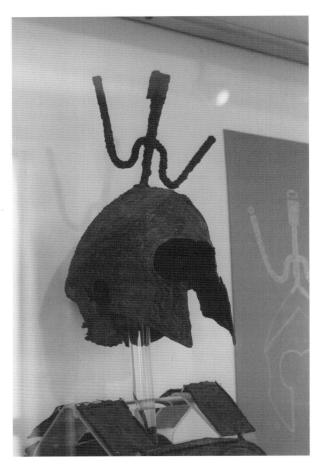

main groups each with its own territory – the Carricini, Caudini, Hirpini, and Pentri – to whom we should probably add the Frentani. But these Oscan groups often formed new tribal configurations. In the late 5th century BC a new Oscan-speaking people, the Lucanians (Lucani), emerged – perhaps as a southern offshoot from the Samnites; and in the middle of the following century another Oscan-speaking people, the Bruttians (Bruttii) split off from the Lucanians in the toe of Italy.

THE GREEKS

Beginning in the 8th century BC, Greeks began to plant colonies along the Italian seaboard. The earliest, on Pithekoussai – now Ischia in the Bay of Naples – was founded initially by Greeks from Euboia as an offshore haven for Greek merchants and carriers following the coastal route to trade with Etruscan clients. But from the late 8th century other Greek settlements were founded on the fertile coastal plains of southern Italy and Sicily so as to relieve population pressures back home, and these became sources of wheat, olives and wine for the mother-cities. These colonies were politically autonomous from their cities of origin, though they normally retained close cultural and sentimental links.

Attic helmet, *c.* 400 BC, from Paestum. With good ventilation, hearing, and vision without sacrificing too much facial protection, this was a popular style, especially with *equites* and *velites*. Improved versions appeared, with a cranial ridge for better protection and hinged cheek-pieces for better ventilation. This Lucanian example is complete with holders for a horsehair crest flanked by feathers. (Gaudo Tomb 136; photo Fields-Carré Collection)

CELTIC INCURSIONS

Italy in the Late Iron Age was thus a melting pot of different ethnic and tribal groupings. When Rome was an immature republic, the brew was violently stirred up by the arrival in the peninsula of migrating Celts from west-central Europe, where the La Tène chiefdoms had emerged perhaps around 500 BC. In the period from about 400 BC Celtic tribes (Boii, Insubres, Senones and others) moved south across the Alps and colonized the Po valley, which they seized from the Etruscans. From there they carried out forays into the heart of the peninsula, far to the south. It was a band of such Senones Gauls which in 390 BC marched down the Tiber to inflict a crushing defeat on the Romans and to loot and burn the city. Legend has it that the Capitoline hill held out, but this is probably patriotic myth, and the Romans were still obliged to buy off the invaders with a humiliating ransom. These southerly incursions were mostly carried out with the object of plundering portable goods (wealth was measured in gold and cattle), or securing prisoners for ransom or for sale as slaves. These were highly mobile pillagers whose sole objective was to capture as much as they could and then head for home with the fruits of their summer's plundering as the rains of autumn set in. However, Gallic warriors were always respected as fearsome fighters, and some remained behind to seek their fortune as mercenaries, especially with Rome's Greek neighbours in southern Italy.

THE AGE OF KINGS

As far as we can tell, the earliest government of Rome comprised a king (*rex*) with military, religious and political power (*imperium*); a consultative council (*senatus*) of elders (*patres*) drawn from the chieftains of the ruling clans (*gentes*); and a consultative assembly (*comitia curiae*) constituted on a federal basis from the various hamlets (*curiae*). These kings, at least two of whom are said to have been Etruscans, were not hereditary monarchs, each king being inaugurated by the consent of the gods and the acclamation of the people. Also, while kings fought and kings fell, the *senatus* or Senate lived on.

Around 625 BC, Rome was politically unified by creating a single central marketplace, the *forum Romanum* or Forum, and locating there certain communal buildings such as the shrine of Vesta and a palace, the Regia (later the seat of the *pontifex maximus*). Also the hamlet system was dissolved by creating three tribes: the Ramnes, Tities and Luceres – all Etruscan names, and thus ostensibly evidence of the influence of Rome's powerful northern neighbours. These were not based on residence or ethnic origin, and the inhabitants of Rome therefore became one people – Roman citizens.

CLAN WARFARE

Before Rome was drawn into the Etruscan orbit to become part of an urbanized region its wars appear to have been characterized by raid, ambuscade and rustling, with perhaps the occasional pitched fight between armies. The latter

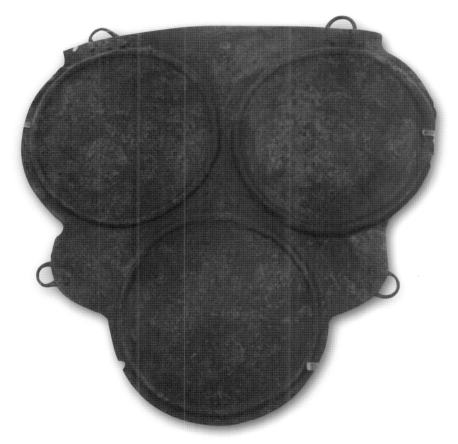

Early Italic armour consisted of single circular pectoral and back plates, some 20–24cm (7–9in) in diameter, and was the basis of this type of Oscan armour. Affording a greater degree of protection than its rudimentary predecessor, the triple-disc cuirass consisted of three symmetrical bronze discs placed on the chest and the back, joined by linked rectangular shoulder and waist plates. This example from Paestum, *c.* 400 BC, belonged to a Lucanian warrior. (Gaudo Tomb 136; photo Fields-Carré Collection)

The Etruscans were the most cultured of the Italic races; both politically and militarily Rome borrowed much from Etruria, and at least two of its seven kings were said to be Etruscan. These two Etruscan warriors wear Etrusco-Corinthian helmets; this Italic pattern was developed from the Corinthian type much used by Greek hoplites, and retained the eye-holes and nasal guard for decoration. Note, at left, the muscled cuirass. (Detail on 3rd-century BC alabaster cinerary urn; Palermo, Museo Archeologico, 8461; photo (Fields-Carré Collection)

were little more than war bands formed by a warrior aristocrat, his kinsmen, friends and clients, such as the clan gathering of the Fabii with its '306 clansmen and companions' (Livy 2.49.4) who marched to fight against Veii, Rome's Etruscan neighbour across the Tiber. Though friends and clients extended the natural limits of a clan these war bands could not have exceeded a few hundred men at most, and in most cases far fewer, because of the economic and logistical constraints inherent in the subsistence-type economy over which Romulus' village presided. Even if this exact figure cannot be accepted at face value, a raiding force of some 300 warriors would be fast, versatile and predatory, and could cause considerable damage and terror. In short, military matters during this pre-urban period were on a very modest and personal basis; the clan chieftain fought for personal glory, his followers out of loyalty to him and in the hope of having that loyalty rewarded with portable loot.

Plundering was a normal part of Roman warfare, and these chieftains probably arose from among the 'big men' common to war-band cultures –

FROM WAR BAND TO PHALANX

During Rome's 'age of kings', there was no appreciable military difference between the Romans and their neighbours. Rome's population and territory were not large, and the communities that they raided and were raided by in turn were often barely a day's march away. A clan chieftain would collect the warrior-farmers of his own family and clients into a war band, taking rations with them for the two or three days that the raid might last. Collectively they might make one or two such raids per season, so it would not impose a great strain on farming manpower or food stocks. With a national levy specially mustered and led by the king himself the scale increased, to the point where it was possible to fight pitched battles and pillage whole regions rather than merely hamlets and homesteads. The Roman concept of an organized army evolved during the so-called 'Servian' reforms, which introduced a census of citizens and military obligations classified by age and wealth. Although now a 'nation in arms', this enlarged force was still made up of citizen-farmers, who could afford to spend only a few summer weeks on the campaign trail before they need to return to their fields.

As a result conflicts were of short duration, usually decided by a single head-on collision between opposing forces.

Here we imagine such a battle, between (**left**) the war band of an Italic people and (**right**) a Roman army in phalanx formation, depicted so as to dramatize the difference between the old and new methods of warfare. The war-band leader (**It L**) is depicted in the type of 'Villanovan' bronze harness revealed by archaeological finds throughout central Italy. So too is one of the few wealthy warriors in his following, contrasted with an impression of the much more numerous common clansman (**It W**). The warriors have no formed order, and their clan and family leaders have a purely inspirational role in battle. The war gear of the Roman leader (**RL**) and of the 'class I' citizens in the front two ranks of the phalanx (**R1**), shows the strong Graeco-Etruscan influence of this period, though the slung pectoral and dorsal plates typical of early Italic warriors were still to be seen. The class II and class III citizens (**R2** & **R3**) making up the third-fourth and fifth-sixth ranks of the phalanx show decreasing amounts and older styles of armour, and are protected mainly by the large *scutum*; the class IV men in the rear ranks (**R4**) have no helmets or armour.

RL

R4

R3

R2

R1

It L

It W

Funerary painting from Paestum depicting a Lucanian horseman returning victorious from battle. He carries on his left shoulder a *tropaion*, trophy, with a 'flag' and a 'streamer' attached. In fact these are a bloody tunic and an Oscan belt, the spoils stripped from a dead or captured enemy. The horseman wears an Attic helmet adorned with horsehair crest and two feathers – see also helmet on page 12. (Andriuolo Tomb 86, *c.* 330/320 BC; photo Fields-Carré Collection)

restless and charismatic types who made good mainly through the redistribution of the surplus wealth that military success could bring. While this remote period lies almost outside recorded history and such deeds went unwritten, it is likely that the adventures of bold and generous warriors were passed down and embellished by bards. Destitute as they are of historical credibility, many of the heroic tales of early Rome recorded by Livy (*History of Rome*, Books 1–3) may have their origins in the panegyric oral poetry composed to celebrate hawkish achievements during this turbulent time of borderland forays.

The predatory and opportunistic behaviour of these early Romans is ideally illustrated by the flurry of raids and counter-raids conducted against the local mountaineers – the Sabini, Aequi and Volsci – during what Livy labels as frequent instances of *nec certa pax nec bellum fuit* – 'neither assured peace nor open war' (2.21.1). Clearly he is putting literary flesh on legendary bones with his many tales of battles fought, chieftains slain, villages pillaged, strongholds besieged and fields burned. In this tribal – as opposed to state – warfare there were battles but no campaigns, tactics but no strategy, and the role of war-band leadership was largely inspirational. Despite the emphasis on crops and cattle, however, we should resist the conclusion that these inter-tribal hostilities were for economic motives. While all these tribes assumed that victory would bring some sort of material benefit, the underlying cause of conflict was to avenge wrongs and to uphold honour in something resembling internecine blood-feuds. In economic terms predation was a totally unproductive activity, since it merely moved to and fro the fruits of other tribes' labours.

Early Roman warfare, a virtually unbroken continuum of thatch-burning and cattle-lifting, was not an exclusively élite pastime. The heroic virtues

of prowess, courage and generosity, an insatiable desire for fame and an overwhelming fear of disgrace, acted to strengthen the social and cultural underpinnings of a nascent Rome struggling to define itself and gain a foothold amongst its powerful neighbours, setting standards of conduct by which all its warriors were to be judged. This created a predatory form of society, with power becoming centralized in the strong right arms of a select few – men more inclined to the sword than the ploughshare.

CITY-STATE WARFARE

Hard times make hard men, and Romulus – the name-giver, outcast and fratricide – was supposed to have welcomed all comers to his foundation. And so the first Romans were a motley bunch, like their leader himself – refugees from the social and physical margins. A notable theme of the stories of early Rome is its willingness to accept outsiders, something that was certainly rare amongst the Greeks, for instance; and even the famous theft of the Sabine women ended in peace between hostile neighbours (Livy 1.9.1– 13.8). When a neighbouring community was destroyed its land was acquired by Rome, and the conquered villagers were often taken to Rome. Such villages often gained security by yielding before attack, the population becoming the clients of the king or some clan.

All the kings (except Tarquinius Superbus) increased the size of Rome both in area and population (Livy 2.1.2). Yet membership of Rome was not simply a status that one did or did not possess; it was an aggregate of rights, duties and honours that could be acquired separately and conferred by instalments. Those populations seen as ethnically and linguistically close to

In 390 BC, Rome was sacked by Gallic Celts led by Brennos, a shadowy figure in history but no doubt dreadfully real to the inhabitants of the city. The Italic peoples were initially terrified by the tall, strongly-built Gauls, who adorned themselves with torques, sported long moustaches, stiffened their hair with lime, and are often depicted as fighting naked. The Gauls' path to Rome led through the Etruscan communities of the Po valley; this stele of c. 400 BC shows an Etruscan horseman encountering a Gallic warrior. The rider appears to be wearing a linen corselet cut in the Greek style, with *pteruges* below the waist and tied-down shoulder doubling, but reinforced with metal scales. (Bologna, Museo Civico Archeologico; photo Ancient Art & Architecture)

A central factor in the 'Servian' reforms of the 5th–4th centuries BC, ascribed by Roman tradition to Servius Tullius, was the constitutional innovation of the census, which divided citizens into property classes. In this much later 1st-century BC sculpture from the Altar of Domitius Ahenobarbus, a clerk records names during either a census or the levying of citizen-soldiers. (Paris, Musée du Louvre, Ma 975; photo Fields-Carré Collection)

Rome were eventually admitted to full Roman citizenship, while to those less close a sort of half-citizenship, under Latin law, was sometimes offered. On the sites of former settlements or on unsettled land garrison colonies were planted, either Roman (*coloniae civium Romanorum*), in which case they were peopled with Roman citizens, or Latin (*coloniae Latinae*), with some autonomy but fewer rights. Another possible status was that of ally, *socus*, with or without treaties granting equal rights but still with obligations.

Thus Rome began its long career of conquest and control through a commonsense policy of incorporation, gradually absorbing all its nearby rivals and growing, and as it grew so too did the scale of its conflicts. Raiding and plundering were still common, naturally, but there was a shift towards pitched battles, which required far greater military organization and resources. The choice of military response to win or protect territory was now to be a civic matter, and the war bands and their heroic chieftains were replaced by a wider levy of all those adult males who could provide themselves with the appropriate war gear. Hence the adoption of the Greek-style phalanx,

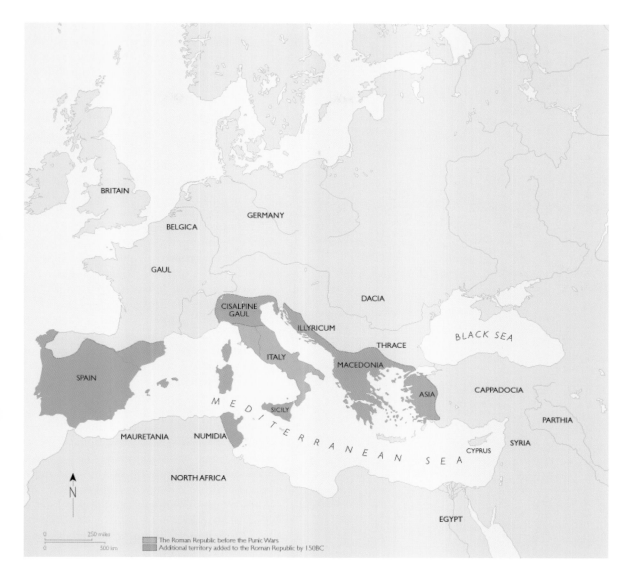

The Roman Republic before the Punic Wars

Additional territory added to the Roman Republic by 150 BC

composed of citizens wealthy enough to outfit themselves with the full panoply of a hoplite, armoured spearman. Though it is said (e.g. Diodoros Siculus 23.2.1) that the phalanx came by way of the Etruscans – an argument that plays up the native Italic tradition – in all probability it owed its origins to the Greek cities that fringed the coasts of southern Italy.

THE 'SERVIAN' ARMY

Livy (1.42–43) and the Greek historian Dionysios of Halikarnassos (4.13–23), both writing in Rome under Augustus (r. 27 BC–AD 14), attribute a major reform of Rome's socio-political and military organization to the popular king Servius Tullius (r. *c.* 579–534 BC). His project for the creation of a citizen army depended on inducing citizens to arm themselves adequately, so a census of all adult male citizens recorded the value of their property and divided them accordingly into classes. Whether or not Servius actually existed, archaeology does suggest that the Romans adopted hoplite panoply at around this time,

so the annalistic tradition may be broadly accurate. The reform scarcely sprang complete from the head of Servius, but its principles belong to this period, while its details were elaborated only over years of gradual development.

In Livy (1.42.5–14), the Servian 'class I' essentially fought with hoplite panoply, each man equipping himself with bronze helmet, corselet and greaves, and the *clipeus* – the *aspis* carried by Greek hoplites, a dish-shaped shield approximately 1m (36in) in diameter and clamped to the left arm. Weapons were spear and sword. Men of class II equipped themselves similarly but were not expected to provide a corselet, while those of class III could omit the greaves as well; however, to balance the absence of body armour classes II and III used the oval *scutum* instead of the round *clipeus*. This was a body shield, Italic in origin, very much like the *thureos* ('door-like') item common to peltasts of later Hellenistic armies. Finally, classes IV and V were armed as skirmishers, the latter perhaps carrying nothing more than a sling. It has been suggested that there were in fact two stages of development here: first a single undifferentiated class, *classis*, of those who possessed the minimum qualification to serve as hoplites, with all the rest named *infra classem*, and later a fivefold subdivision.

More important was the subdivision of these five classes into centuries, *centuriae*. In each class half the centuries were made up of older men (*seniores*, those from age 47 to 60), obviously more suitable for garrison duty, and half of younger men (*iuniores*, those from 17 to 46). The centuries in each class were unequal in number, as the state naturally drew more heavily upon the well-equipped wealthier men than on those lower down the property ladder. Thus class I contained 80 *centuriae*; classes II, III and IV, 20 each; and class V, 30 centuries. Below them were five *centuriae* of unarmed men, four of artisans and one of *proletarii*, whose property was too little to justify enrolment in class V. Known as *capite censi*, 'counted by heads', these men were simply counted and had no military obligations, no political rights and no tax liability (in other words, poverty – curiously, perhaps, to our modern eyes – freed men from conscription). At the opposite extreme were those who served on horseback, the sons of the well-to-do making up 18 *centuriae* that took precedence over the centuries of the other five classes.

Italic votive bronze plaque, 5th century BC, depicting a warrior bearing a *clipeus*. The rest of his hoplite panoply consists of a crested Italic 'pot' helmet, Graeco-Etruscan greaves, and two spears, one apparently with a larger head than the other. Spearheads have been found in a range of shapes and sizes. (Atestino, Museo Nazionale; photo Fields-Carré Collection)

5th-century BC Italic Negau helmet, a bronze bowl-shaped skull with a ridge running fore-and-aft and a lateral depression at its base; it had no cheek-pieces, and was held in place by a leather chin strap. Developed in the 6th century from the Italic 'pot' helmet, the Negau pattern remained in use unchanged down to the 3rd century BC. (Arezzo, Museo Archeologico Nazionale; photo Fields-Carré Collection)

Under the Republic this system would provide the basis of the *comitia centuriata*, the 'assembly in centuries' at which the citizens voted to declare war or accept peace; elected the consuls, praetors and censors – the senior magistrates (i.e. posts with *imperium*) of Rome; and tried capital cases. Gathering on the *campus Martius* or Field of Mars, an open area outside the original boundary of the city, the structure of the assembly exemplified the ideal of a militia in battle array, with men voting and fighting together in the same units. This assembly operated on a 'timocratic principle', the common idea whereby the property-owning classes lived in a 'stakeholder' society, where political rights were defined by military obligations, which in turn sprang from the need to defend property, with property itself giving the financial means to engage in that defence. The idea was that those who have property, and thus a stake and a role in the defence of society, are considered more likely to take sensible decisions about how the state is run; the richer you are the truer this becomes, and conversely, having nothing to lose will make you irresponsible. The timocratic principle meant that only those who could afford arms could vote, so the *comitia centuriata* was in effect an assembly of property-owning citizen-soldiers. Oddly enough, however, the 'Servian' army of Livy and Dionysios does not appear in their respective battle accounts.

optiones

principes

signiferi

1

2

3

G+S
E

The wealthiest citizen-soldiers of early Rome stood in the foremost ranks of the phalanx and wielded the *hasta,* exemplified by this 5th-century BC Etruscan bronze spearhead. It has a leaf-shaped blade with a midrib, and a closed socket; the midrib gives greater longitudinal strength to a spearhead, increasing its effectiveness at piercing shields and armour. (Arezzo, Museo Archeologico Nazionale; photo Fields-Carré Collection)

THE AGE OF CONQUESTS

However it came about, the phalanx was concomitant with the rise of poorer but focused and highly competitive societies, city-states in which the hoplite was a citizen of some property. The new weaponry and tactics meant more bloodletting. However, it also allowed for a high measure of decision by battle – certainly a prerequisite for outnumbered but well-organized citizen-soldiers – and for successful territorial expansion, as in the case of Rome. Once encouraged, Roman expansionism progressed in three stages: the conquest of Italy (400–270 BC), the conquest of the western Mediterranean (270–200 BC), and the conquest of the Greek world (200–146 BC). The first stage was formative.

It was during the 4th century BC, in the course of interminable warfare with its hostile neighbours, that Rome – originally no different from the other, relatively tiny city-states of central Italy – developed its singular military culture. Once the pattern was established it fed on itself. As soon as a large part of the Italian peninsula had been brought into the Roman confederacy the drive to expand became irreversible, because that confederacy, like

B MANIPULUS IN BATTLE ARRAY

Note: in this and the following plates, the use of colours to distinguish the *hastati* (yellow – **3**), *principes* (blue – **2**) and *triarii* (red – **1**) is purely diagramatic, not historical.

The term *manipulus*, 'a handful', derived from the handful of straw suspended from a pole as a military standard, and hence meant soldiers belonging to the same unit. With the adoption of the manipular legion the maniple became the basic fighting unit of the Roman army, organized into two centuries (*centuriae*). Each maniple carried its own standard (*signum*), and each *centuria* was led by a centurion (*centurio*). Each centurion was supported by four subordinates: a second-in-command (*optio*), standard-bearer (*signifer*), trumpeter (*cornicen*) and guard commander (*tesserarius*). The standard-bearer and trumpeter must have stood close to the centurion to hear his commands, and the *optio* stood at the rear of the *centuria* to keep the men steady and in place. The *tesserarius* supervised the posting of the nightly sentries and was responsible for distributing the daily watchword, which he received inscribed on a token (*tessera*). Polybios writes that centurions 'choose from the ranks two of their bravest and most soldierly men to be the standard-bearers for each maniple' (6.24.5); as there was only one *signum* per maniple, however, one of the *signiferi* was evidently a substitute should anything befall the other. He also says each maniple had two *centuriones* so that the unit 'should never be without a leader and commander' (6.24.6). As the maniple rather than the century was the tactical unit, the *centurio prior*, the first of the

two to be appointed, was responsible for commanding the maniple as a whole in battle, the *centurio posterior* only taking over if the senior man fell.

Centurions were either appointed by the military tribunes or elected from amongst the ordinary soldiers (*milites*). They were usually chosen from experienced and proven soldiers, steady rather than especially bold men, but they had to be literate. Though centurions were of the same social background as the men they led, the senior centurion of the legion, commander of the first maniple of the *triarii* and ranked *centurio primi pili*, was included *ex officio* along with the tribunes in the consul's war-council. Such men might be very experienced indeed.

With 60 heavy legionaries to a *centuria* there are only three practical formations: in files three deep, six deep, and 12 deep, each formed by halving the frontage of the previous formation. We show the second, with spacing of about one pace between files and about two paces between ranks, giving a century a frontage of about 18 metres and a depth of at least 12 metres (or 6 metres, for the smaller *centuria* of *triarii*). The basic six-ranks-by-ten-files formation is confirmed by the normal marching order of six abreast. When the 20 *velites* light skirmishers attached to each *centuria* are added, we arrive at the standard of eight men to a file (cf. Greek system of using multiples of eight). Known as a *contubernium*, 'a tentful', the members of a file shared a tent, and living in close proximity for long periods would have promoted solidarity and comradeship – what modern academics call 'small-group dynamics'.

Negau helmet and Graeco-Etruscan greave from a 5th-century BC tomb at Brisighella, Ravenna; although Umbrian in context, such equipment would not look out of place in the 'Servian' phalanx of early Rome. The use of items of Italic armour hardly affected the function of the Greek-style phalanx so long as the front-rank soldiers bore the *clipeus*. (San Martino Tomb 10; photo Fields-Carré Collection)

everything else about Rome, was geared for war. The Italian allies, the *socii*, rendered to Rome only military service, not tribute; the fact that this was all Rome could demand of them provided an additional incentive to war, since this was the only way that Rome could profit from its alliances. By the beginning of the 3rd century BC the Romans had brought most of the Italian peninsula into their confederacy, giving it the largest manpower reserves in the western Mediterranean, and the habits of more or less constant war had become ingrained.

The second stage brought the two Punic wars against Carthage (264–241 BC, 218–201 BC), and the Roman conquest of the western Mediterranean coasts and neighbouring islands. There has been much debate over the causes of the First Punic War, all of it well-rehearsed in print, but in the long view it does not seem to matter much what made the Romans cross the narrow straits into Sicily. The essential fact is that the venture represented the first departure from

Etruscan horseman depicted on a 3rd-century BC alabaster cinerary urn. He wears a crested Etrusco-Corinthian helmet with cheek-pieces, and a linen corselet cut in the Greek style with tied-down shoulder doubling and *pteruges*, reinforced with metal scales – see also the much earlier relief on page 17. He holds the cavalry shield adopted from the Greeks and is armed with a sturdy spear. Since Rome lacked a tradition of horsemanship most of her cavalry was provided by *socii* allies. (Palermo, Museo Archeologico, 8462; photo Fields-Carré Collection)

traditional Roman policy, which had never looked beyond the Italian mainland, but that once the Romans found themselves on the island, they stayed there. Rome managed to convert itself into a naval power, withstood appalling losses, and fought for more than 20 years until Carthage conceded. Here we witness the real secret of Rome's success: its willingness doggedly to persist in warfare year after year. When the war was over Rome absorbed the Carthaginian overseas territories and became a western Mediterranean power. The second round, the war with Hannibal – the most titanic conflict yet seen in the west – did nothing more than confirm this conclusion, and provide an even more impressive demonstration of the invincible tenacity of what we regard as the Roman war machine.

The via Appia, built in 312 BC on the initiative of the censor Appius Claudius Caecus. This road made it easy for Roman troops to move between Rome and the new conquest of Capua. Initially 211km (130 miles) long, the road was later extended to Brundisium via Tarentum. (Fields-Carré Collection)

The socii

As well as citizens Rome could call on allied troops, at first from its Latin neighbours and later from all over Italy. While they struggled to obtain mastery of the peninsula the Romans had two codes for dealing with peoples who opposed them. If the enemy resisted them stubbornly, so that the Romans had to take the place by storm, then the whole community might be enslaved and their homes destroyed. But if they submitted to the besieging commander in good time – normally, before the first scaling ladders were placed against their walls – then their fate was decided by the Senate.

In the light of experience, the Senate invariably chose the course of binding Latin and Italian communities to Rome by a series of bilateral treaties – a multi-tiered system of control that operated by the time-honoured principle of 'divide and rule'. Such treaties specified that an allied community must contribute a certain number of troops to aid Rome in time of war, and in return allowed them a share in any booty. Otherwise the ally paid no tribute to Rome and was free to pursue its own cultural agenda. The durability of the arrangement is famous, and here we should note the great difficulties Hannibal experienced in detaching Rome's Italian allies when campaigning on the peninsula.

The allies fell into two broad groups: Latin and Italian. The *socii nominis Latini*, 'allies of the Latin name', included a handful of old communities that had not been granted citizenship after Rome's defeat of its insurgent allies in 338 BC, as well as Latin colonies strategically sited throughout Italy. These communities were collectively capable of producing 80,000 foot and 5,000 horse, according to Polybios (2.24.10), and the greater part of Rome's army was either Roman or Latin. The other allies were Italians of various nations – in the same passage (2.24.10–13) Polybios mentions, among others, the Sabines, Etruscans, Umbrians, Samnites and Lucanians – who could collectively provide another 170,000 foot and 30,000 horse. All allies were theoretically obliged to help Rome with their total manpower, but in practice their obligations may have been defined by what was known as the *formula togatorum*, 'list of adult males' – a kind of sliding scale of the numbers of men required according to the number of citizen-soldiers raised in any year (Brunt 1971: 545–548).

Many of the Latin colonists were in fact descended from Roman citizens, men who had accepted Latin status in place of Roman citizenship in order to make a fresh start (Livy 27.9.10–11). Thus the culture of such colonies was virtually identical to that of Rome, and they enjoyed certain rights under Roman law. On the other hand, Rome's Italian allies were a diverse group, being geographically, ethnically, culturally, politically and often linguistically distinct. They were in theory independent, but in fact Rome was clearly the dominant partner in such alliances.

By 201 BC Rome may have been prepared to halt; the Senate seems to have been genuinely reluctant to enter the alien and complicated Greek-speaking world to the east. It is doubtful that any Romans at that time had any ambitions for, or concept of, world empire, whether in terms of military *realpolitik* or the romantic mentality of Virgilian-style poetry. All its traditions rooted Rome in Italy; to hold down a fringe of seaboard and islands in the western Mediterranean did not detract from the Italo-centric nature of Roman policy. These overseas possessions provided generals with opportunities for easy triumph-hunting among ill-organized 'barbarians', but the Hellenistic world was another matter: over there, those in power were kings who ruled vast territorial kingdoms.

For half a century Roman policy toward the Greeks alternated between sudden destructive intrusions and long periods of withdrawal, but the mechanisms of expansion in Roman society were still running and would not allow Rome to withdraw completely. During these intrusions the Roman military system, tempered in the struggle with Hannibal, won decisive victories over the Hellenistic kingdoms at Kynoskephalai (197 BC), where the army of

Philip V of Macedon was made to look somewhat ridiculous, and Magnesia (190 BC), where Scipio Africanus and his brother Lucius triumphed over the juggernaut of Antiochos III of Syria. A later intrusion destroyed, utterly and permanently, the Macedonian army on the field of Pydna (168 BC), and left Rome without rivals (Dawson, 1996: 116–118).

Thereafter, Rome was what the Greeks called the *hêgemôn* of the known world, and the Greeks, by expecting Rome to act like a hegemonic power, pulled the Romans ever deeper into their labyrinthine affairs. Simultaneously a kind of military professionalism had come into being, in which the lure of spoils, the desire for glory and the opportunities of an ever-increasing reservoir of manpower all played their part. In a revealing comment, Polybios (32.13.6–8) reports that the Senate feared the Roman army would lose its fighting edge if it were not used. It is argued (Harris, 1986) that the temptation to exercise power by despatching forces to the next place, and then the next, was almost irresistible; by the mid-2nd century BC Romans were becoming accustomed to the idea of empire in the east, and felt no more inhibitions about annexing territory there.

With an awful inevitability, the process was completed when an example was made by destroying Corinth, almost gratuitously, in the very year that Carthage was wiped from the land of the living.

After the expulsion of the king and his family, Rome was attacked (and probably taken) by Lars Porsenna, a chieftain of Clusium. This Etruscan backlash gave rise to the most famous tales of Roman heroism, such as Horatius Cocles and his lone defence of the bridge, as shown in this fanciful 19th-century Italian engraving. Horatius still remains one of the best-known figures of the young Republic. (Ancient Art & Architecture)

THE MANIPULAR LEGION: LIVY AND POLYBIOS

We have two accounts of the manipular legion's organization. First, the Roman historian Livy, writing more than three centuries after the event, describes the legion of the mid-4th century BC. Second, the Greek historian Polybios, living and writing in Rome in the mid-2nd century BC, describes the legion of his time. The transition between the Livian and Polybian legion is somewhat obscure.

In his account of the year 340 BC, after the close of the First Samnite War and as a preamble to the Latin War, Livy (8.8.3–8) offers a brief description of Roman military organization. Introduced as part of the Servian reforms, the legion had originally operated as a unified hoplite phalanx. More recently, however, the Romans had adopted manipular tactics, whereby the legion was now split into distinct battle lines.

Behind a screen of light-armed troops (*leves*), the first line contained maniples (*manipuli*) of *hastati* ('spearmen'), the second line was made up of maniples of *principes* ('chief men'), and the third line, made of the oldest men, consisted of maniples of *triarii* ('third-rank men'). One significant problem with Livy's account, however, is the fact that he has 15 maniples in each of the three lines, as opposed to Polybios' ten maniples. Other groups, whom Livy calls *rorarii* and *accensi*, were lightly equipped and drawn up behind the *triarii*, and it is from the definitions compiled by the Roman scholar Varro (*De lingua Latina* 7.57–58) that we can identify the *rorarii* as skirmishers and the *accensi* as servants.

Despite its anomalies, Livy's account is pleasingly close to that given by Polybios, and almost certainly derives from it. Its independent value, therefore, is not great, and, if we choose to follow Dionysios of Halikarnassos, Livy places the manipular system too far back in time by suggesting that the phalanx was abandoned by Rome after its ten-year duel with nearby Veii. In contrast, Dionysios says 'cavalry spears' (20.11.2), i.e. hoplite spears, were still employed in battle by the *principes* during the war with Pyrrhos (280–275 BC). It is therefore reasonable to speculate that the evolution from hoplite phalanx to manipular legion was a slow and gradual business, which for Livy was a process completed by the turn of the 4th century BC. For the organization of the legion, *terra firma* is reached only with Polybios himself.

Polybios breaks off his narrative of the Second Punic War at the nadir of Rome's fortunes, following the three defeats of the Trebbia, Lake Trasimene, and Cannae, and turns to an extended digression on the Roman constitution (6.11–18) and the Roman army (6.19–42). For us the latter is of inestimable value, not least in that it is written by a contemporary, himself a former cavalry commander (*hipparchos*) in the Achaean League, who had seen the Roman army in action against his fellow-countrymen during the Third Macedonian War (172–168 BC), and had perhaps observed its levying and training during his internment in Rome (167–150 BC).

All citizens between 17 and 46 years of age who satisfied the property criteria – i.e. who owned property above the value of 11,000 *asses* – were required by the Senate to attend a selection process, *dilectus*, on the Capitol. Although Polybios' passage (6.19.2) is slightly defective here, citizens were liable for 16 years' service as a legionary, *miles*, or ten for a horseman, *eques*. These figures represent the maximum total time that a man could be called upon to serve. In the 2nd century BC, for instance, a man was normally expected to serve up to six years in a continuous term, after which he expected to be released from his military oath. Thereafter he was liable for recall as an *evocatus* for up to his maximum limit of 16 years or campaigns. Some men might serve for a single year at a time, and were expected to present themselves again at the next *dilectus*, until their full six-year period of continuous service was completed.

At the *dilectus* the citizens were separated by age and height, and brought forward four at a time to be selected for service in one of the four consular legions being raised for that year's campaign. The junior military tribunes of each legion took it in turns to choose men, to ensure an even distribution of experience and quality. The recruits then took a formal oath; Polybios does not give an exact text, but writes that the soldier swore that 'he would obey his officers and carry out their commands to the best of his ability' (6.21.1). To speed up the process one of a number of men swore the oath in full and the rest assented to it, perhaps saying *idem in me*, 'the same for me'. They were then given a date and place to muster, and were dismissed to their homes.

The Polybian legion consisted of 1,200 *hastati* in ten maniples of 120; 1,200 *principes* organized in the same way; and just 600 veteran *triarii*, in ten smaller maniples. Polybios, like Livy, writes that the *hastati* were the men in the flower of their youth and strength; the maturer *principes* were in the prime of manhood; and the *triarii* were veterans. The same order for the three battle lines appears in Polybios (14.8.5, 15.9.7), in Livy (30.8.5, 32.11, 34.10), and in other antiquarian sources (e.g. Varro, *De lingua Latina* 5.89).

Foreshortened view of a Greek *kopis*, 4th century BC. The secondary weapon of a hoplite, this was a single-edged blade that widened towards the point, thereby increasing the kinetic energy of a downward cut. Its hilt, in the form of a horse's head, curves back to guard the knuckles. This example is richly decorated with silver inlay; the missing insets from the hilt would have been bone or ivory. (Madrid, Museo Arqueológico Nacional; photo Fields-Carré Collection)

This 19th-century Italian engraving imagines the duel fought between champions of Rome and Alba Longa. Each side fielded triplets, and initially things went badly for Rome when two of the Horatii were cut down by the Alban Curiatii. However, the survivor Horatius retreated until his three wounded opponents had split up and then slew each in turn. (Ancient Art & Archaeology)

THE ROMAN WAY OF WAR

THE WAR BAND

Among the legacies that the Romans bequeathed to modern man is the fully developed practice of war, yet in the very beginning their way of war was little different from that practised by other Italic peoples. In the manufacture of arms, in military tactics and in economic and social development Rome and its neighbours were all closely similar. Their war bands met quite frequently on the field of conflict, in shifting alliances and hostilities, and any such technical developments would quickly have been copied or shared.

At the apex of a definite societal pyramid was the individual clan chieftain, and next to him were his own close relatives. Next came more distant relatives and friends, and finally a broad base consisting of clients –

C **BATTLE ARRAY WITH *VELITES***
Of the 4,200 legionaries in a legion, 3,000 were heavy infantry. The remaining 1,200 men, the youngest and poorest, served as light infantry and were known as *velites*, 'cloak-wearers'. However, it is important to remember that the distinction between what Graeco-Roman authorities label 'heavy' and 'light' infantry was not so much a reference to their lighter equipment as to the fact that the former were trained to fight together in formation, and the latter as skirmishers. Generally skirmishers operated in a very loose order, with wide gaps between men to ensure that they could easily move to avoid incoming missiles. The loose and fluid formation thus employed allowed each man great freedom to advance and retire at will.

For administrative purposes, the *velites* were divided among the legionaries of the maniples, each maniple being allocated an equal number. Normally, *velites* would open a battle screening their heavier comrades; after withdrawing through their ranks they would regroup on the *triarii*, and then either remain in reserve or threaten the enemy's flanks.

They appear not to have had their own officers, being commanded by the centurions leading the maniples, yet they could be quite effective in battle, and probably relied on 'natural leaders' for tactical command. Livy (31.35.4–6, 38.21.12–13) describes them successfully skirmishing from a distance by throwing their javelins and then fighting at close quarters with their swords, using their shields to protect themselves. Polybios (6.22.3) mentions that certain *velites* would wear a wolfskin over their helmets and shoulders so that they would be visible to their centurions from a distance; such individuals, being keen to impress, could well have led by example. A high degree of courage would have been required in order to get close enough to hit the enemy, entering the 'killing zone' and exposing the individual to enemy missiles. Thus, the main importance of preliminary skirmishing was probably moral or psychological. Ancient writers regarded this initial phase of battle as inconclusive and tactically insignificant, and it is quite likely that comparatively few casualties were inflicted or suffered.

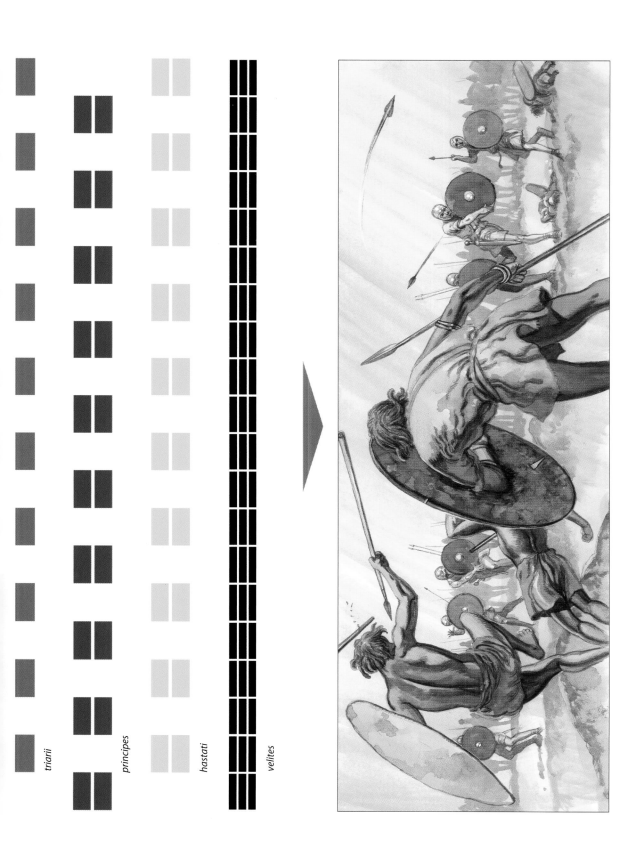

triarii

principes

hastati

velites

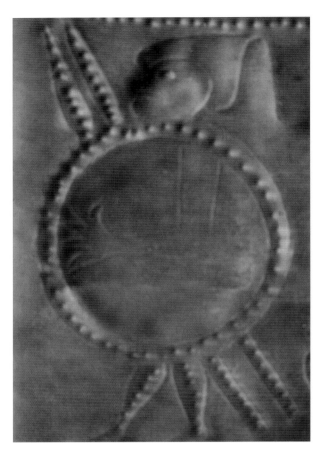

Italic votive bronze plaque, 5th century BC, showing a Venetic warrior carrying two long spears and a large round shield, the *clipeus*. He wears a Villanovan helmet of antique pattern; the join of the two-part skull was decorated with a tall, standing, arrowhead-shaped plate. Of no practical value, this solid crest did make the wearer appear taller and thus more frightening. (photo Fields-Carré Collection)

dependants who stood in a filial relationship to the clan chieftain. As patron he granted protection, and in return the client was expected to render certain services, of which the most important was joining the patron's war-party for a predatory excursion, so that fame and loot would accrue to chieftain and clan alike.

Any accurate portrayal of early Roman battle tactics presents a challenge. The heroic-style literature of Livy offers little insight into actual manoeuvres, although a few details do stand out in the hot chaos of his battle scenes, and so we assume that the social structure of an army was reflected in its behaviour on the field of battle. With their world centred on the clan, bound together by kinship and ruled by its chieftain, warfare for the Romans probably consisted of two types of activity: single combat and group combat.

To continue on this speculative road – for we have none other to follow – we may suggest that a clan chieftain owed his position to the fact that in time of war he fought with conspicuous courage, demonstrating the heroic ideal by stepping out in front of all others to challenge, fight and defeat an enemy chieftain under the eyes of friend and foe alike – we should not think of him as holding back, judiciously overseeing the action from behind the battle line, monitoring developments and despatching terse messages to subordinates. Competition, especially in the close-quarter climax of battle, presented him with the opportunity to acquire or reinforce the prestige and legendary status that he needed to strengthen and maintain his pre-eminent position. In an age when intellectual pursuits were poorly regarded, leadership tended to be physical, robust and violent. The bearing of arms, especially a long-bladed sword for slashing, may have been regarded as a potent symbol – first, of free manhood, and second, of power and wealth. Clan chieftains rose and fell by the casual brutality of the sword, and on some occasions single combats might be formally arranged with the opposition. For instance, we read that the three Roman Horatii brothers – triplets – fought as champions against the three Curiatii brothers – also triplets – of next-door Alba Longa. According to Livy's swashbuckling account (1.23–25), two of the Roman champions were quickly cut down, but not before they had wounded their Alban opponents. The last Horatius then pretended to flee, drawing the wounded Curiatii into pursuit until they had separated, at which point he turned upon them and despatched each one separately with his sword.

When the common clansmen were drawn into a general fight we may assume that there were few niceties of tactics, just a sprawling scuffle and scramble as men of each side hammered away at each other until exhaustion or weight of numbers swung the balance. Uniformity was never a characteristic of the war band, and the quality and quantity of weapons and equipment would vary widely, from the abundant to the minimal. Archaeology allows us to say with some confidence that men of lesser means were without armour and almost certainly equipped with a shield, throwing-spears, and hand weapons such as daggers or axes. Grave-goods evidence reveals that the sword was the least common of hand-weapons, and thus presumably associated with the wealthier or more successful members of a clan. In contrast, the spear and shield were plentiful, being made largely of wood, which was cheap and readily available. If a clansman's war gear consisted of a two-spear set and a shield, then we can infer that one of the spears was thrown as a missile weapon, and the other retained for stabbing once the opposing sides had closed on each other.

Against this array of offensive weaponry the clansman entrusted his safety first and foremost to his shield, which was in all likelihood the Italic *scutum*. The central circular hole through which the horizontal handgrip was fixed was protected by a metal boss plate, which could be used as an offensive weapon. With the exception of a few of the wealthiest warriors body armour was not worn, and metal helmets were rare. Caps at least of *cuir bouilli*, boiled leather, were used, and anything else that would protect the head could have been pressed into service, such as wickerwork reinforced with discs of bronze, and each individual would bring whatever he could afford or could scrounge. For the most part, however, the only things that prevented a clansman's death or serious injury in the hurly-burly of battle were his *scutum*, and his own courage, physical strength and agility.

The composition of armies may have varied according to their function (e.g. cross-border raiding, or a levy for home defence), but each would

Stele from Tarquinia, 7th century BC. Whereas clansmen were best equipped for and accustomed to cattle-raiding and skirmishing, hoplites were armoured spearmen who fought shoulder-to-shoulder in the phalanx. These citizen-soldiers were now protected by helmet, corselet and greaves, all of bronze, and wielded a long spear and large shield. (Monterozzi Tomb 89; photo Fields-Carré Collection)

Tufa cinerary urn from Volterra, 2nd century BC; part of the relief depicts two Etruscan warriors, one bearing a *scutum* (right) and the other a *clipeus* (left). Both these shield types were used in the Greek-style phalanx of early Rome, the *clipeus* by citizen-soldiers of class I and the *scutum* by classes II and III. (Florence, Museo Archeologico, 5744; photo Fields-Carré Collection).

optiones

decuriones

optiones

decuriones

normally have consisted of an agglomeration of war bands fighting under the command of, and loyal to, individual clan chieftains, while the army as a whole might have been under the aegis of the king himself. As the leader of his people the king had a solemn obligation to protect them against the depredations of their neighbours and to lead them on expeditions of plunder and conquest. For the conduct of such warfare he was undoubtedly empowered to summon the clan chieftains and their followers to a mustering. These clan gatherings were disbanded at the end of a military operation, and the clansmen went back to work on the land until the need next arose.

As time went by and kingship became increasingly centralized, there was probably a gradual decline in the independence of clan chieftains and a corresponding rise in the king's power over them. Then, as the state became more powerful than the individual clans of which it was composed, war bands were superseded by what we recognize as a state-sponsored army. It has been suggested that the first Roman military organization was based on the three tribes of the late regal period, the Ramnes, Tities and Luceres. Each tribe furnished 1,000 men towards the army, under the command of a *tribunus*, tribal leader; and each tribal unit was divided into 100-man sub-units, *centuriae*, under the command of a *centurio*, 'leader of one hundred'. The resulting force, some 3,000 men all told, was known as the *legio*, the levy, and in essence represents Rome's earliest conventional army. The nobility (or their sons) now made up a small body of cavalry, about 300 horsemen drawn equally from the three tribes. The battlefield role of these *equites* is obscure; they may primarily have formed the king's personal bodyguard rather than playing a major part in battle tactics.

D. CAVALRY *TURMA* IN BATTLE ARRAY

The cavalry (*equites*) formed the most prestigious element of the legion, and were recruited from the wealthiest citizens able to afford a horse and its trappings. These formed the top 18 centuries of the voting assembly (*comitia centuriata*), and were rated *equites equo publico*, obliging the state to provide them with the cost of a remount should their horse be killed on active service. Marcus Porcius Cato – Cato the Elder – boasted that his grandfather had five horses killed under him in battle and replaced by the state (Plutarch *Cato major* 1.3). Being young aristocrats who knew how to ride, the *equites* were enthusiastic and brave, but better at making a headlong charge on the battlefield than patrolling or scouting. This was a reflection of the lack of an equestrian tradition in Rome, as well as the fact that the *equites* included the sons of many senators, eager to make a name for courage and so further their future political careers.

Each legion had about 300 *equites* organized into ten *turmae*, and to each *turma* the military tribunes appointed three *decuriones*, of whom the senior commanded with the rank of *praefectus*. Each *decurio* chose an *optio* as his second-in-command and rear-rank officer. While exact numbers would vary over the course of a campaign, this organization suggests that the *turma* was divided into three files of ten, each led by a *decurio*, 'leader of ten', and closed by an *optio*. These files were clearly not tactical sub-units, for the *turma* was evidently intended to operate as a single entity, as indicated by the seniority of one *decurio* over his two colleagues. Here we show

two possible formations: (**top**) deployed for battle and (**bottom**) for movement before deployment.

The cavalry of the *ala* – the 'wing' of *socii* allied troops – was generally two or three times more numerous than that of the *legio*. The *socii* were organized in *turmae* of probably the same strength as the *equites*, and presumably also came from the wealthiest strata of society. This is certainly suggested by Livy's references (23.7.2, 24.13.1) to 300 young men of the noblest Campanian families serving in Sicily, and to the young noblemen from Tarentum who served at Lake Trasimene and Cannae. Allied cavalry were commanded, at least from Polybios' day, by Roman *praefecti equitum*, presumably with local *decuriones* and *optiones* at *turma* level.

Cavalry served primarily to protect the flanks of the consular army. The cavalrymen of the two *legiones* are usually depicted as stationed on the right wing, the position of honour, whilst those of the two *alae* formed on the left; however, given that there were at least twice as many of the latter as the former, this may be an oversimplification. Combat between cavalry invariably took place on the margins of the battlefield, flanking the general infantry contest. Under normal circumstances one side would apparently have been intimidated by the other and given way before colliding with them. This seems reasonable, for horses will not charge into an impenetrable object, and a steady body of enemy horsemen in close formation might well have been perceived as such. Steady cavalry nearly always relied upon moral rather than physical shock to cause the enemy to flinch, break and run.

THE PHALANX

We have 4th-century BC carved ivory plaques from Palestrina (ancient Praeneste, 17.5km (11 miles) east of Rome) that depict two armoured spearmen each wearing a muscled cuirass over a thigh-length tunic, under a cloak fastened at the throat. Their Attic helmets have fore-and-aft horsehair crests, and greaves and a pair of spears complete their panoply. It appears that each of them has a large round shield propped against his left leg. Since these men would not look out of place in a phalanx – the word means 'stacks' or 'rows' of fighting-men – the plaques are a reflection of the new tactics of Roman citizens fighting in formation.

Warriors are not soldiers. Both can be courageous killers, but disciplined soldiers value the group over the single heroic individual, and can operate en masse as a collective whole. Clan warfare, with its ancient allegiances of kinship, had given rise to confrontations and duels characterized by individual fervour. For this reason the advent of the Greek-style hoplite phalanx, with its armoured spearmen standing shoulder-to-shoulder, changed the very nature of combat: individual exploits were replaced by corporate actions, and in Rome the archaic clan-warrior became a disciplined citizen-soldier.

Throughout history the use of spear and shield have been inextricably linked, and for this new style of spear/shield warfare the weapon *par excellence* of the hoplite was the long thrusting spear (Greek *doru*, Latin *hasta*). Fashioned out of ash wood and some 2–2.5m (6½ft to 8½ft) in length, the spear was equipped with a bronze or iron spearhead and a bronze butt-spike. As well as acting as a counterweight to the spearhead, the butt-spike allowed the spear to be planted in the ground when a hoplite was ordered to ground arms (being bronze, it did not rust), and gave him a secondary blade to fight with if his

Hoplite phalanx; scene from the Nereid monument, dated *c.* 400 BC. In the front rank, fifth from the left, is a hoplite with his head turned to the right. He may be a general encouraging his fellow citizens as they advance into contact. Phalanxes were calibrated by the depth of their cumulative shields – 'eight shields deep', 'twelve shields deep' etc – not by counting spears. (London, British Museum, 868; photo Fields-Carré Collection)

These 4th-century BC ivory plaques from Palestrina give a good impression of the war gear of an early Roman soldier. Much of it is Graeco-Etruscan in style, and each of these men, armed with a pair of spears, appears to have a *clipeus* resting against his leg. They would not have been out of place in the foremost rank of the 'Servian' phalanx. (photo Fields-Carré Collection)

spear snapped in the mêlée. The weapon was usually thrust overarm at the face of the foe, although it could easily be thrust underarm if the hoplite was charging into contact. The centre of the shaft was bound in cord for a secure grip.

The hoplite shield (Latin *clipeus*) had a wooden core – usually of some flexible wood such as poplar or willow – faced with a thin layer of stressed bronze and backed by a leather lining. Because of its great weight the shield was carried by an arrangement of two handles: an armband in the centre through which the forearm passed, and a handgrip at the rim. Held across the chest, it covered the hoplite from chin to knee, but since it was clamped to the left arm it only offered protection to his left-hand side. It was the hoplite shield that made the rigid phalanx formation viable. Half the shield protruded

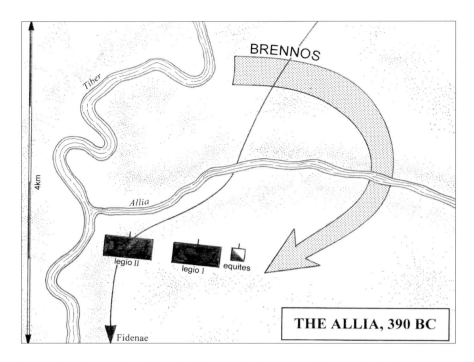

THE ALLIA, 390 BC

beyond each man's left-hand side, and if the next soldier to the left moved in close his uncovered right side was protected by the overlap. Hence, hoplites stood shoulder-to-shoulder with their shields locked. Once this formation was broken, however, the advantage of the shield was lost; as Plutarch says (*Moralia* 241), the body armour of a hoplite might be for the individual's protection, but his shield protected the whole phalanx.

The phalanx itself was a deep formation, normally composed of hoplites 'stacked' in files eight to 12 men deep. In this dense mass only the front two ranks could use their spears offensively, but the men in the third and subsequent ranks added weight to the attack, probably by shoving the men in front with their shields. Thucydides (4.43.3, 96.4) and Xenophon (*Hellenika* 4.3.19, 6.4.14), Greek authors who had first-hand experience of hoplite battle, commonly refer to the push and shove of a hoplite mêlée.

In hoplite warfare, therefore, tactics were largely limited to the clash of two mutually opposing phalanxes. The crucial battle would usually be fought on flat ground with mutually visible fronts that were no more than a kilometre (1,000 yards) or so long, the adversaries being drawn up often only a few hundred metres apart. Normally, after a final blood-sacrifice to the gods, the two opposing phalanxes would simply head straight for one another, breaking into a trot for the last few paces, colliding with a crash, and then – drunk with adrenalin and blinded by the dust – stabbing and shoving until one side cracked. The mêlée itself was a horrific, toe-to-toe affair, the front two ranks of opponents attempting to stab their spears (kept sharp by constant whetting) into the unprotected throat or groin of the men facing them, inflicting immediately or ultimately fatal injury. Meanwhile, the ranks behind would push. As may easily be imagined, once a hoplite was down, injured or not, he was unlikely ever to get up again, and the man behind simply had to step forward over him to maintain the integrity of the rank. This short but vicious mêlée was resolved once one side had practically collapsed. There was no pursuit by the victors, and those of the vanquished who were still able fled the field of slaughter.

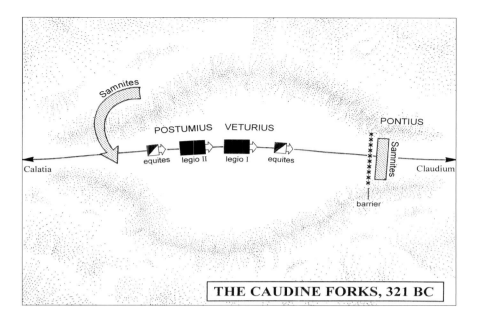

THE CAUDINE FORKS, 321 BC

Phalanx versus war band

An important part of the story of Rome is the long series of wars by which it subdued the peoples of Italy. Initially, the Romans were preoccupied with the circle of tribes in their immediate neighbourhood: the Etruscans to the north, the Latins to the south, and the Volsci and Aequi to the south-east and east. However, these adolescent steps of conquest were arrested by the land-hungry Gauls who, having spilled over the Alps and settled in the Po valley, launched plundering raids deep into the Italian peninsula. On the banks of the Allia (390 BC), a tributary of the Tiber just 11 Roman miles (16.25km) north of Rome, the Senones utterly defeated the army sent to repel them (Livy 5.38), and the city itself was sacked. Fortunately for the Romans, however, these Gauls were primarily out for plunder rather than territory, and promptly withdrew northwards laden with their loot.

A more challenging opponent lurked closer to home. The Samnites were perfectly capable of mobilizing themselves and federating into a league when they needed to fight. The Romans faced the Samnites in long, savage wars,

Funerary art from Paestum, c. 330 BC: a battle scene depicting two hoplite phalanxes about to clash head-to-head. The one on the left is largely obscured by damage; that on the right is believed to be the winning side, as it is led by a heroically nude figure in the act of thrusting with his spear – perhaps to be identified with an Italic Mars. The shields show individual blazons. (Andriuolo Tomb 114; photo Fields-Carré Collection)

Some of the many iron *pilum* heads and foreshafts recovered from Telamon, scene of a decisive victory over the Gauls in 225 BC; they may have been deposited as a votive offering in a local temple. The surviving lengths range between 190mm and 350mm (*c.* 7½–13½in), and these would have been fastened to a one-piece wooden shaft, generally of ash. The fixing method, as seen here, was the double-riveted tang. The head itself was clearly designed to puncture shield and armour, the foreshaft passing through the hole made by the head. (After Vacano, 1988, abb. 5, taf. xi)

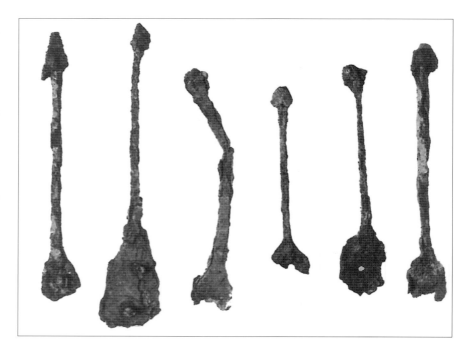

and sometimes suffered serious reverses, as at the Caudine Forks (321 BC). It appears that the Romans had been attempting to adopt a more pugnacious stance against the Samnites, combining the forces of both consuls and advancing into the territory of the Caudini, the southernmost of the Samnite tribes. Livy writes (9.2.5) that the Romans were on their way to Apulia, but alternatively this may have been an attempt to knock the Caudini out of the war. Whatever their intentions, the Romans advanced into the valley of the Caudine Forks, where they found the way blocked with a defended barricade of felled trees and boulders. On trying to disengage they discovered that the entrance to the narrow defile had also been blocked with its own defended barricade, and after vain attempts to cut their way out the consuls surrendered to avoid starvation. The entire army suffered the humiliation of being forced by their victors to 'pass under the yoke' – a frame made from two spears stuck in the ground with a third lashed across horizontally at a height that compelled the Roman soldiers, disarmed and clad only in a tunic, to crouch down to pass underneath. This disaster was to be the last time that Rome accepted peace as the clear loser in a conflict. War, post-Caudine Forks, was to be a life-or-death struggle that could only end in one of two ways. The first was for the enemy to cease to be a threat, either because they had become a subordinate ally of Rome or because they had ceased to exist as a political entity; the second was for Rome itself to cease to exist.

THE MANIPULAR LEGION

The next stage in the development of the Roman army, which falls after the regal period and during the early Republic, is associated traditionally with the name of Marcus Furius Camillus, a national hero credited with saving Rome from the Gauls and commemorated as a second founder of Rome. These military reforms fall under three headings: first, the introduction of a daily cash allowance, the *stipendium*, for soldiers; second, the adoption of the *scutum* instead of the *clipeus* as the standard shield, while the *pilum* throwing-spear was substituted for the *hasta*; and finally, the replacement of the phalanx by the manipular legion. Two *legiones* were created, each of 3,000 legionaries and each commanded by a consul (Livy 1.43.1, 5.7.5, 8.8.3; Plutarch *Camillus* 40.4).

That all these major changes were effected at the same time and under the guidance of one quasi-legendary man is improbable. Though the long siege of Veii may well have necessitated the provision of pay to allow the soldiers to meet their living expenses while away from home for an increasingly lengthy period, the adoption of new equipment and a new tactical formation was much more probably the result of experience gained from a series of campaigns. The Italic oval shield, the *scutum*, was already being carried by some of the soldiers at this date, while some of them continued to be armed with the *hasta* for another 200 years or more. Further, it has been suggested that the *pilum* was copied by the Romans from their Samnite enemies (e.g. Sallust, *Bellum Catilinae* 51.38), or alternatively they may have developed it from a more rudimentary weapon of their own. Then again, the *gladius* was probably forged on Iberian models, and may have been seen first in the hands of Iberian mercenaries employed by the Carthaginians during the First Punic War. When all is said and done, it is likely that a whole series of piecemeal reforms was later lumped together and attributed to the wisdom of Camillus, who was the period's most famous general.

This was a period when Rome was a young republic, feeling its way and still a little unsteady on its feet. Nonetheless, when the Greeks of Neapolis (modern Naples) appealed to the Romans for aid against the Samnites, who had occupied and garrisoned their city, Rome accepted what became the Second Samnite War (327–304 BC). Described by Livy (Books 7–10) in his entertainingly dramatic style, this conflict was particularly hard fought, and – as described – the Roman army suffered a humiliating reverse at the Caudine Forks in 321 BC. Rome soon broke the unfavourable treaty that followed this disaster, resuming the struggle in 316 BC, and despite a number of further setbacks the city at length emerged triumphant.

This was a war of attrition, and the adaption of the hoplite phalanx into the manipular legion may have been prompted through bitter experience of fighting in the rough, mountainous terrain of the central Apennines. In this sort of country armies were constantly at the mercy of ambushes, supply failures, missed rendezvous, or the rash over-stretching of the line-of-march (as at the Caudine Forks). The Roman phalanx might defeat the mountain men of Samnium on the plains, but in their own highlands they presented a far greater challenge. Military history offers no place of education as unforgiving as the battleground, so there can be little doubt that it was in these campaigns of attrition that the Romans learned more pliant tactics.

The *triplex acies*

The legion was essentially a development of the phalanx. The Romans articulated the single block into three lines, *triplex acies*, with each line in turn broken up into small blocks capable of independent manoeuvre, with enough space between the soldiers to allow them to use their weapons effectively. By the time of Hannibal most soldiers were armed with *pilum* and *gladius*, but the third line retained the longer *hasta*. These blocks (*manipuli*) were each made up of two *centuriae* (centuries), the administrative sub-units of the legion, but the *manipulus* was the basic tactical unit in the Roman battle line. It was under the command of the *centurio prior*, the senior of the two centurions, who could be replaced at need by the junior, the *centurio posterior*.

The Romans thus sacrificed the depth and cohesion of the phalanx for mobility and flexibility. They sent the three lines of maniples into the attack in turn, the legionaries of the first two casting their *pila* and running to meet the enemy head-on with their *scuta* and *gladii*. In their combined use of *pilum* and *gladius* the Romans had partly solved the age-old dilemma of choosing between missile- and shock-attack. When combat is reduced to its simplest elements these are the only two methods by which an enemy can be defeated on the battlefield: the shock attack seeks to annihilate him in hand-to-hand struggle, and the missile attack aims to destroy or drive him away before he can come to close quarters, by the attrition of a constant and deadly sleet of missiles. Legionaries hurling their *pila*, albeit at close range, matched the offensive punch of missile troops, and with their *scuta* and *gladii* they served as shock troops. Moreover, two lines of maniples to the rear – those of the *principes* and *triarii* – watched the initial engagement of the first line of *hastati*, ready to exploit success or prevent collapse.

Battle would be opened by the screening *velites*, light infantry skirmishers who attempted to disorganize and unsettle enemy formations with a scattering of missiles, each individual carrying a clutch of javelins to be thrown in quick succession. This done, they retired through the gaps between the maniples of the *hastati* and made their way to the rear. The line of *hastati* now re-formed to close the gaps, either by each maniple extending its frontage, thus giving individuals more elbow-room in which to handle their weapons, or – if the maniple was drawn up two centuries deep – by the *centurio posterior* moving his *centuria* to the left and forward, to form up alongside the *centuria* of the *centurio prior* in the front line (Keppie, 1998: 38–39).

E **LEGIO IN BATTLE ARRAY**

(1) The 'Polybian' legion consisted of five elements – the heavy infantry *hastati*, *principes*, and *triarii*; the light infantry *velites*; and the cavalry *equites*. Each was equipped differently and had a specific place in the legion's tactical formation. Its principal strength was the 30 maniples of its heavy infantry, the *velites* and *equites* acting in support of these. Its organization allowed it only one formation: the *triplex acies*, with three successive, relatively shallow lines of ten maniples each. These fighting units, supporting each other to apply maximum pressure on an enemy to the front, were in simple terms divided 'horizontally' into three lines, and 'vertically' into maniples. When deployed, each maniple may have been separated from its lateral neighbour by the width of its own frontage (c. 18m), though this is still a matter of some debate. Livy tells us simply that the maniples were 'a small distance apart' (8.8.5). Moreover, the maniples of *hastati*, *principes* and *triarii* were staggered, with the more seasoned *principes* covering the gaps between the *hastati* in front, and likewise the veteran *triarii* covering those between the *principes*. Modern commentators call this formation the *quincunx*, from the five dots on a dice-cube.

The legion was a force designed for large-scale battles, for standing in the open, moving straight forward and smashing its way frontally through any opposition. Polybios (2.24.13, 6.20.9) puts its nominal strength at 4,200 legionaries; however, in times of particular crisis larger legions were raised, as was the case at Cannae, and the number might be increased to as many as 5,000. He says (6.21.9–10) that when this happened the number of *triarii* remained the same at 600, but the number of *hastati*, *principes* (and *velites*) – the less experienced legionaries – increased from the usual 1,200; consequently the size of a maniple of *hastati* or *principes* could step up from 120 to 160 men. Of course, this applied when a legion was first formed, and before its numbers were whittled away by combat deaths, injuries, disease and desertion.

(2) After the *velites* had withdrawn through the gaps the maniples of *hastati* would naturally have to re-form to close the gaps before advancing to contact. If the gap really was equal to the frontage, and the maniple was drawn up two centuries deep, the *centurio posterior* might move his *centuria* to the left and forward, to form up alongside the *centuria* of the *centurio prior* in the front line (Keppie, 1998: 38–39).

(3) The classic sequence of advancing to hand-to-hand contact: first light and then heavy *pila* are thrown, then the legionary draws his *gladius* and rushes at the enemy facing him, punching with his *scutum* and stabbing around its edge.

1

enemy

2

3

The *pilum*

The first line now walked slowly forward in an eerie silence until some 15 metres from the contact point – the effective range of a *pilum*. Immediately and without warning the *hastati* then let fly their missile weapons, throwing first their light and then their heavier *pila*. Even if these did not actually impale the enemy, the *pila* would often become embedded in their shields, the barbed points making them difficult to withdraw and their weight making the shield extremely unwieldy; additionally, the thin metal foreshaft often bent on impact, thus preventing the weapon being thrown back.

During the confusion caused by this *pila* storm, which could be devastating, the *hastati* drew their swords and 'charged the enemy yelling their war cry, and clashing their weapons against their shields as is their custom' (Polybios 15.12.8, cf. 1.34.2). He also writes (18.30.6–8) that the Romans formed up in a much looser formation than other heavy infantry, adding that this was necessary for the soldier to be able to use his sword and to defend himself all round with his shield. This implies that the legionary essentially fought as an individual swordsman during the confusing but hopefully decisive end-phase of battle.

The *gladius* and *scutum*

In his brief description of the *gladius Hispaniensis* (Greek *Iberikós*), Polybios writes that it was an excellent weapon 'for thrusting, and both of its edges cut effectually, as the blade is very strong and firm' (6.23.6–7). He evidently states that it was 'worn high on the right thigh' so as to be clear of the legs – a vertically-hung scabbard would normally be impractical for walking, let alone for fighting. The wearing of the sword on the right side goes back to the Iberians, and before them to the Celts. The sword was the weapon of the aristocratic warrior, and to carry one was to display high status. It was probably for cultural reasons alone, therefore, that the Celts carried the long slashing sword on the right side rather than on the left – the side covered by the shield – which meant that the weapon was hidden from view. But if, at this early date, the legionary already carried his sword on his right hand side suspended from a waist belt, it would not be for any cultural reason. As opposed to a single scabbard-slide acting as a pivot at the top, the more stable four-ring suspension system on his scabbard enabled the legionary to draw his weapon quickly with the right hand, an asset in close-quarter combat. In view of its relatively short blade, inverting the hand to grasp the hilt and pushing the pommel forward enabled him to draw the *gladius* with ease. With its sharp point and firm four-ring suspension arrangement, the Delos sword, confidently dated to 69 BC, shows all the characteristics of the *gladius* described a century earlier by Polybios. Another such example is the Mouriès sword, found in a tomb in association with a group of pottery and metal artefacts; this assembly can be dated to around the beginning of the 1st century BC (Bishop-Coulston, 1993: 53; Feugère, 2002: 79).

Polybios, in an excursion dedicated to the comparison between Roman and Macedonian military equipment and tactical formations, states that 'According to the Roman methods of fighting, each man makes his movements individually: not only does he defend his body with his long shield, constantly moving it to meet a threatened blow, but he uses his sword both for cutting and for thrusting' (18.30.6). It appears, therefore, that the tactical doctrine commonly associated with the Roman legion of the Principate was already in place during Polybios' day. We know from archaeological data that the *gladius* of the Principate ('Pompeii' type) was an amazingly light and well-balanced weapon that was capable of making blindingly fast attacks, and was suitable for both cuts and thrusts. However, Tacitus (b. *c.* AD 56) and Vegetius (fl. *c.* AD 385) both lay stress on thrusting rather than slashing; the latter rightly says that 'a slash-cut, whatever its force, seldom kills' (1.12). Having thrown the *pilum* and charged into contact, the standard drill for the imperial legionary was to punch the enemy in the face with the shield-boss and then stab him in the belly with the razor-sharp point of the sword (Tacitus *Annales* 2.14, 21, 14.36, *Historiae* 2.42, *Agricola* 36.2).

In his near-contemporary account of the battle of Telamon (225 BC), Polybios tells us that 'Roman shields... were far better designed for defence, and so were their swords for attack, since the Gallic sword can only be used for cutting and not for thrusting' (2.30.9). Of a battle of 223 BC he writes that legionaries 'made no attempt to slash and used only the thrust, kept their swords straight and relied on their sharp points... inflicting one wound after another in the breast or the face' (2.33.6). In a much later passage (6.23.4) he implies that they were trained to take the first whirling blow of the Celtic slashing-sword on the rim of the *scutum*, which was suitably bound with iron (the principal weakness of a wooden shield was that it could be split in two with a well-aimed sword blow, leaving a soldier virtually defenceless).

Slightly foreshortened in this view, an iron sword and dagger from Almedinilla, Córdoba, 4th or 3rd century BC remind us that Iberian straight-bladed weapons were the forebears of the *gladius* and *pugio*, the characteristic trademarks of a Roman legionary for some four centuries. Housed in scabbards, they were hung from a belt using a stable ring suspension system, which was also copied by the Romans. (Madrid, Museo Arqueológico Nacional; photo Fields-Carré Collection)

For maximum protection the legionary scrunched up tight behind his *scutum*, and the use of the thrust also meant that he could keep most of his torso well covered even during weapon-play. The *scutum*, having absorbed the attack of his antagonist, was now punched into his face as the legionary stepped forward to stab with his *gladius*; much like the riot-shield of a modern policeman, the *scutum* was used both defensively and offensively, to deflect blows and to hammer into the opponent's shield or body to create openings. As he stood with his left foot forward a legionary could get much of his body weight behind this punch, added to the considerable weight of the *scutum* itself. Each legionary had about a metre within which to fight, perhaps twice as much elbow-room as a soldier of the Macedonian phalanx (who, armed with a long pike-like *sarissa*, depended on the mass and density of his formation to roll over the opposition). Meanwhile, the legionaries in the second rank stood behind the intervals between the men in the first, ready to protect their comrade's flanks and to step up to replace them when they tired or fell.

Ideally, the *hastati* fought the main enemy line to a standstill, but if they were rebuffed or lost momentum an entire second formation, the succeeding line of *principes*, surged forward into the combat zone, casting their *pila* over their comrades' heads in the mêlée, and the entire process of well-drilled butchery could begin anew with fresh troops. In the meantime, the *triarii* watched and waited at the rear. Close-quarter hand-to-hand fighting was physically exhausting and emotionally draining, and the skill of a Roman commander lay in committing his second and even third lines at the right moments. If he left reinforcement too late the fighting line might buckle and break, but if he ordered it too soon the value of adding fresh soldiers to the mêlée might be wasted. Obviously, the survivors of the *hastati* and the *principes* reinforced the *triarii* if it came down to a final trial of strength. The phrase *inde rem ad triarios redisse*, 'the last resource is in the *triarii*' (Livy 8.8.9), passed into Latin usage as the byword for a desperate situation.

Victory would eventually go to the side that endured the stress of staying so close to the enemy for the longest and was still able to urge enough of its men forward to renew the fighting. According to Polybios' measured analysis, it was the inherent flexibility of the manipular system that made the legion so formidable:

> The order of battle used by the Roman army is very difficult to break through, since it allows every man to fight both individually and collectively; the effect is to offer a formation that can present a front in any direction, since the maniples that are nearest to the point where danger threatens wheel in order to meet it. The arms they carry both give protection and also instil the men with great confidence, because of the size of the shields and the strength of the swords, which can withstand repeated blows. All these factors make the Romans formidable antagonists in battle and very hard to overcome. (15.15.7–10)

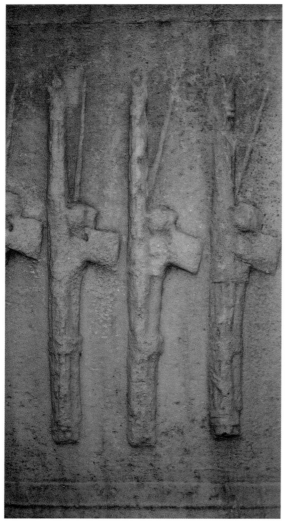

Imperium was symbolized by the magistrates' lictors, who each carried an axe, *securis*, enclosed in a bundle of rods, *fasces*, which thus indicated that their master could decree both capital and corporal punishment. Four such badges of office decorate this tombstone of a former consul. (Naples, Museo Archeologico Nazionale; photo Fields-Carré Collection)

Hellenistic armies, for instance, preferred to deepen their phalanx rather than form troops into a second line, and made little use of reserves, as the commander's role was usually to charge at the head of his cavalry in the manner of Alexander the Great. The deepening of the *sarissa*-armed phalanx gave it great stamina in the mêlée, but even the men in the rear ranks were affected by the stress and exhaustion of prolonged combat. The Roman system, by contrast, allowed fresh men to be fed into the fighting line, renewing its impetus and leading a surge forward that might well be enough to break a tired enemy. In battle physical endurance is obviously of the utmost importance, but all soldiers in close contact with danger become emotionally even if not physically exhausted as the battle proceeds. When writing of ancient warfare, Colonel Ardent du Picq notes that the great value of the Roman system was that it kept only those units that were necessary at the point of combat, and the rest 'outside the immediate sphere of moral tension' (1946: 53). The legion, organized into separate battle lines, was able to hold one-half to two-thirds of its men outside this zone of demoralization in which the remaining half or third was engaged.

Command and control

Though the two consuls, as the chief magistrates, had a wide range of functions, it was leadership in war that was the core of their year in office, providing both their heaviest responsibilities and their greatest opportunities to win *gloria*, prestige, among their peers. Owing their election primarily to their social standing rather than to any military ability, the consuls usually led an army each: consular legions were numbered *I* to *IIII*, one consul commanding *legiones I* and *III*, the other *legiones II* and *IIII*. An obvious weakness of the system was that while consuls would all have some military experience they often had no experience of command; they were not always chosen for the quality of their generalship, and sometimes displayed such a conspicuous lack of it that Roman armies had to win despite their contributions. Zonaras, a 12th-century AD Byzantine monk, goes so far to claim that the greatest mistake the earlier Romans made was to send out different commanders each year, depriving them command just as they were learning the art of generalship, 'as though choosing them for practice, not use' (8.16). The system was, of course, not the result of a military judgement but a political precaution against the dangerous accumulation of personal power.

Another anomaly to modern eyes is the fact that the legion itself had no overall commander, being officered by six military tribunes, *tribuni militum*. Like the consuls these men were not professional soldiers, but magistrates drawn from the senatorial aristocracy and elected by the citizens in the *comitia centuriata*. Having served a five-year military apprenticeship – normally as *equites* – they would be eligible for election, though ten of the 24 tribunes appointed to the four legions had seen ten years' service (Polybios 6.19.1). The tribunes had a wide range of responsibilities both administrative and tactical, including enrolling and swearing-in new recruits and dividing them into their four categories. They may also have been responsible for training, as well as health and general welfare (Polybios 10.20.1). In the field, tribunes were responsible for the selection of a suitable campsite and the supervision of the camps, and had the authority to punish certain offences by inflicting fines or ordering floggings. Tribunes worked in pairs, each pair commanding the legion for two months out of every six; they drew lots for their turn (Polybios 6.26.9, 34.3, 37.5).

On the battlefield itself the Romans placed great emphasis on encouraging and rewarding individual boldness in soldiers of all ranks, but they also recognized the need for aggressive officers to lead the men into contact. There was an *optio* behind each century to hold the men in place, and a *centurio* in the front rank to urge them onwards. According to Polybios (6.24.9) a centurion was supposed to be selected for his determination and skill as a leader rather than prowess in individual fighting, and stubbornness was especially important. Unlike the centurions, however, the tribunes were not tied to one position within the legion, but would move around the battle line, encouraging the men and committing reserves as necessary.

Mars, god of war, on the Altar of Domitius Ahenobarbus; the deity is depicted in the uniform of a senior officer, probably that of a military tribune. He looks more Greek than Roman, with a crested Etrusco-Corinthian helmet, a muscle cuirass with two rows of *pteruges,* and a cloak. The sash tied high at the waist probably indicated his rank. (Paris, Musée du Louvre, Ma 975; photo Fields-Carré Collection)

MILITIA VERSUS MERCENARY

Rome retained the principle of a militia long after other states in the Mediterranean world had come to rely on soldiers who were mainly professionals. However, the Romans modified their system to cope with the demands of wars that were being fought further and further from home, and the intimate link between warfare and the agricultural year was eventually broken. From the beginning of the 4th century BC, Rome paid its citizen-soldiers for the duration of a campaign (Livy 4.59.11, Diodoros 14.16.5). The wage was not high and certainly did not make soldiering a career, but it covered the citizen's basic living expenses during his military service.

Roman strength lay in the set-piece battle, the decisive clash that settled the issue one way or another. Polybios (1.37.7–10) saw the Romans as rather old-fashioned in their straightforward approach to warfare, commenting that as a race they tended to rely instinctively on 'brute force' (*bía*). No battle illustrates his criticism better than **Cannae (216 BC)**, where Roman tactics subordinated the other arms very much to the heavy infantry, who were to carry the heat and burden of that terrible day. The Roman legions rolled ponderously towards the Carthaginian enemy at a moderate rate, their ranks unusually packed into a close and solid mass. Faced by a vastly more

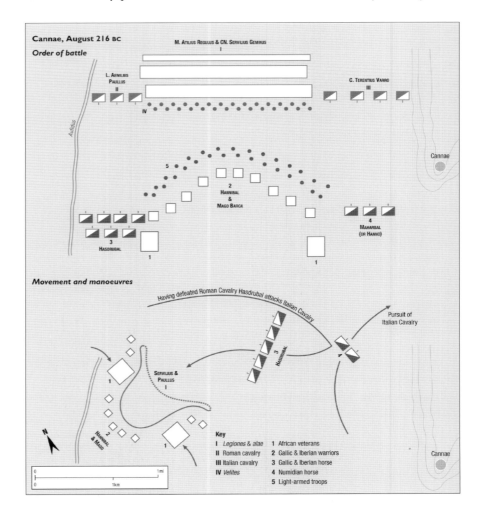

Cannae, August 216 BC

Order of battle

M. ATILIUS REGULUS & CN. SERVILIUS GEMINUS
I

L. AEMILIUS PAULLUS
II

C. TERENTIUS VARRO
III

IV

Aufidus

Cannae

5

2
HANNIBAL & MAGO BARCA

4
MAHARBAL (OR HANNO)

3
HASDRUBAL

1

1

Movement and manoeuvres

Having defeated Roman Cavalry Hasdrubal attacks Italian Cavalry

Pursuit of Italian Cavalry

HASDRUBAL
3

4

SERVILIUS & PAULLUS
I

1

HANNIBAL & MAGO
2

1

N

Cannae

0   1mi
0   1km

Key

I Legiones & alae   1 African veterans
II Roman cavalry   2 Gallic & Iberian warriors
III Italian cavalry   3 Gallic & Iberian horse
IV Velites   4 Numidian horse
                       5 Light-armed troops

numerous army, Hannibal decided, in effect, to use the very strength of the enemy infantry to defeat it, deliberately inviting it to press home its attack on the centre of his line. There his Gauls and Iberians would serve as the bait in the trap, while his Africans formed its jaws. Finally, Hannibal took equal care over the deployment of his cavalry; instead of distributing his horsemen equally between the wings, he placed more against the river on his left. This virtually guaranteed a breakthrough against the numerically far inferior Roman cavalry, and his own horse would then be available for further manoeuvres. The smaller body of cavalry on the open flank, away from the river, were expected to hold the Romans' more numerous Italian cavalry in play for as long as possible. This audacious and immaculately thought-out scheme showed Hannibal's absolute confidence in the fighting abilities of all the contingents of his army. It was well placed, and the Roman army was enveloped and destroyed.

The Romans were naturally appalled when news reached them of the scale of the defeat at Cannae; first reports made no mention of survivors, and the Senate was told that the entire army had been simply annihilated. Not until 14 years later was Rome to exact its revenge. Having invaded North Africa, the brilliant young Publius Cornelius Scipio turned the tables, and Hannibal – the invader of Italy and for 16 years the undefeated antagonist

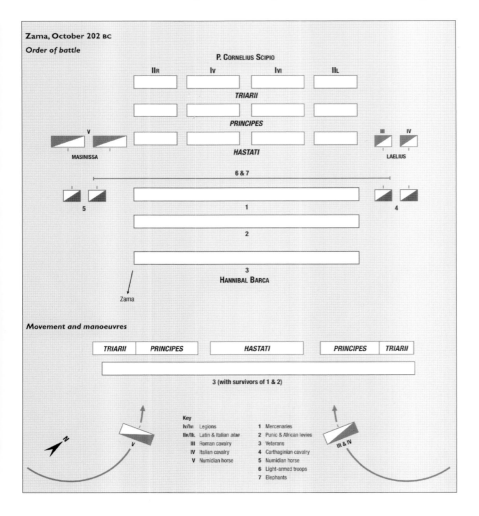

49

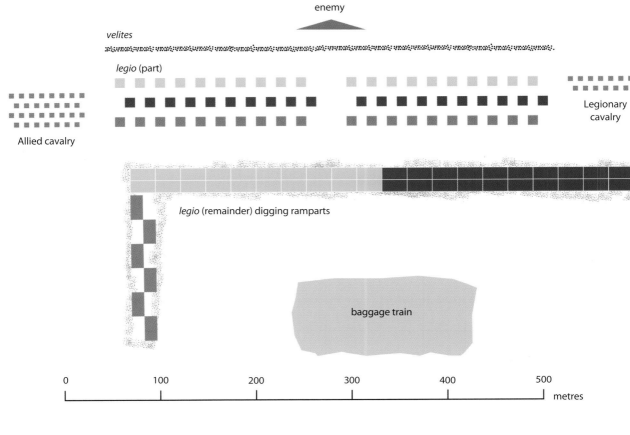

enemy

velites

legio (part)

Allied cavalry

Legionary cavalry

legio (remainder) digging ramparts

baggage train

0	100	200	300	400	500	

metres

enemy →

3.6 m

2.7 m

of Rome – was decisively beaten in modern Tunisia near the small town of **Zama (202 BC)**.

Hannibal had deployed his army in three lines mirroring the Roman array, with the third line, some distance behind the others and in reserve, consisting of his own veterans. These included all the survivors of his Italian army, even some Africans and Iberians who had marched with him from Iberia and Gauls who had joined him in Gallia Cisalpina. In a pre-battle address, Hannibal told these grizzled veterans to remember above all the victories they had gained over the Romans at the Trebbia, Lake Trasimene and Cannae; Polybios emphasises that they were 'the most warlike and the steadiest of his fighting troops' (15.16.4). The cavalry were positioned on either wing, with the elephants and light-armed troops in front of the infantry. For the first time in his career, Hannibal was fighting on ground not of his own choosing and with inferiority in the mounted arm.

During his campaign in Iberia, Scipio had struck up a friendship with a useful Numidian prince, Masinissa, and on African soil this ally's brilliant light horsemen would prove crucial. Scipio stationed Masinissa with his Numidians on the right wing, and his lieutenant, Caius Laelius, with the citizen and allied cavalry on the left wing. In the centre the heavy infantry

CONSULAR ARMY ENTRENCHING

While perhaps not such masters of field engineering as the legionaries of Caesar's army and those of the Principate, nonetheless it was the legionaries of our period who perfected the marching camp. Pyrrhos of Epeiros, an outstanding soldier-of-fortune, is supposed to have realized that he was not dealing with mere barbarians when he saw the order of the Roman camp (Plutarch *Pyrrhos* 16.5). The marching camp gave the men peace of mind, reassuring them that they would have a place of retreat if necessary (although the Romans rarely, if ever, planned to fight from within a camp), and it provided a relatively safe place to sleep. While its defences offered protection only against surprise attack, being sufficient to delay attackers but not to stop them, passing the night behind guarded ramparts prevented any avoidable mental or physical fatigue.

As a consular army neared the end of a day's march one of the military tribunes and centurions who formed the camp surveying team were sent ahead to select a site – open, near water, preferably on rising ground and with no cover that could be exploited by the enemy. The camp itself covered an area about four *plethra* (700m²). A point which afforded maximum visibility was selected for the site of the consul's tent (*praetorium*); a white flag was placed on this spot, and a red flag on the side nearest water. A ditch, some 3 Roman feet (0.9m) deep and 4ft (1.2m) wide, normally surrounded a camp. The spoil was piled up on the inside, faced with turf and levelled off to form a low rampart (*agger*). The two *legiones* constructed the defences at the front and rear of the camp, while the two *alae* built the right and left sides. Each maniple was allotted a working section about 25 metres long. The centurions checked that the work of their maniples was done properly, while a pair of tribunes or prefects supervised the overall effort on each side of the camp (**see figures in bottom image**).

Far stronger defences were needed when camping close to the enemy, when the work might be hampered by attacks. As the army arrived all the cavalry, the light-armed troops and half of the heavy infantry were deployed in battle array in front of the projected line of the ditch facing the enemy (**top**); the baggage train was placed behind the line of the rampart, and the remainder of the soldiers began to dig in (**below**). They dug a ditch 9 Roman feet (2.7m) deep and 12ft (3.6m) wide, piling up the spoil on the inside to form a turf-faced rampart 4ft (1.2m) high. On the march each soldier carried a bundle of sharpened stakes, perhaps prefabricated, perhaps cut from sturdy branches. These were planted close together in the top of the rampart to form a *vallum* or palisade (**see inset**). As work proceeded, the heavy infantry were gradually withdrawn from the battleline, maniple by maniple, starting with the *triarii* who were nearest the rampart, and these soldiers were put to work digging the other sides of the camp. The cavalry were not withdrawn until the defences facing the enemy were complete.

The marching camp was highly organized and uniformly laid out. Always built to recognizably the same pattern, it had four gateways (*portae praetoria*, *principalis dextra*, *decumana* and *principalis sinistra*), and two main roads (*viae principalis* and *praetoria*) running at 90 degrees and meeting in front of the *praetorium*. Between the rampart and the tent-lines was an open area 200 Roman feet (60m) across, known as the *intervallum*, which ensured that the tents were out of range of missiles from outside the defences; more importantly, this space allowed the army to form up ready to deploy into battle order.

Everything was regulated, from the positioning of each unit's tents and baggage to the duties carried out by various contingents; for instance, the *triarii* always provided guards for the horse lines. Likewise, various officers were allocated the responsibilities of supervising the sentries around the camp and transmitting orders for the next day's march.

Military historians regard Cannae as a classic example of a successful double-envelopment manoeuvre. On this hot, dusty, treeless plain, by withdrawing his centre while his wings stood firm, Hannibal annihilated some 50,000 Romans after they were lured forwards between the jaws of the Punic army. This panoramic view of the Cannae battle site was taken next to the 19th-century monument commemorating the Roman disaster. (Ancient Art & Architecture)

were drawn up with the maniples of *hastati*, *principes* and *triarii* one behind the other instead of *quincunx*-fashion, thus leaving lanes to accommodate Hannibal's elephants when they advanced. His *velites* were stationed in these lanes with orders to fall back in front of the elephants or, if that proved difficult, to right and left between the lines.

In the event, a large proportion of the elephants, being young and untrained, were frightened out to the wings, where they did more harm to their own side than to Scipio's, thereby helping the Roman cavalry to sweep their counterparts from the field. The infantry then closed; and after the *hastati*, supported by the *principes*, had broken the first two Punic lines, Scipio redeployed his second and third lines on either wing of the first. Readjustments made, he then closed with Hannibal's veterans, who were also probably flanked by now by the survivors from their first two lines, as Polybios says (15.14.6) that the two forces were nearly equal in numbers. The struggle ended when Scipio's cavalry returned and fell on Hannibal's rear. The mercenaries and levies turned and fled; Hannibal escaped with a small escort, but his veterans, largely armed and equipped in the Roman manner, fought bitterly to the death, pitted against those very legionaries that they had disgraced at Cannae. Without the resources or willpower to continue the struggle, Carthage sued for peace, and the Second Punic War was over at last.

LEGION VERSUS PHALANX

The Macedonian phalanx, unlike the Greek phalanx, was made up of phalangites, soldiers wielding a *sarissa*. In essence this was a pike or elongated spear, varying in length from about 12 to 14 cubits (*c.* 17–21ft). A long shaft of cornel wood was of two-piece construction fitted together with an iron coupling-sleeve; tipped with an iron spearhead counterbalanced by a bronze butt-spike, it weighed about 6kg (13lb). The *sarissa* was held with a two-handed grip about one-third of the way along from the butt, with the other two-thirds – 3.6–4.6m (11–14ft) long – extending in front; this gave the phalangite an advantage in reach over the hoplite spearman of at least 2.4m (8ft).

Used singly, the *sarissa* was a practically useless weapon, since it was too slow and heavy to manoeuvre, but used in conjunction with many others it

Marble bust of Publius Cornelius Scipio Africanus (d. 185 BC). Seeing the deficiencies of the rather static traditional Roman tactics, Scipio experimented with small tactical units that could operate with greater flexibility. His tactics were inspired by Hannibal's, and needed good legionary officers as well as generalship to implement. He thus saw the value of capable subordinates who could proceed on their own initiative. (Rome, Musei Capitolini, MC 562; photo Fields-Carré Collection)

G OVERLEAF: CONSULAR ARMY DRAWN UP FOR BATTLE

By at least the 4th century BC the term *legio*, 'levy', came to denote the most significant subdivision of the army. Later, as Rome's territory and population increased, it was found necessary to levy two consular armies each of two legions. According to Livy (9.30.3), the latest possible date for the regular number of legions to have doubled to four was 311 BC. Polybios (3.109.12) has Rome levying and supporting four active legions of citizen-soldiers each year for annual service, supplemented by an equal number provided by the *socii*.

Thus a standard consular army consisted in its entirety of some 20,000 men. Two *legiones* formed the centre, with two *alae sociorum* deployed on their flanks – these were known as the 'ala of the left' and the 'ala of the right' (Polybios 6.29.9), a positioning reflecting the meaning of *ala*, 'a wing'. Polybios' silence on the subject suggests that the *socii* were organized and equipped along Roman lines, which would certainly have

been desirable for smooth interaction with the *legiones*; presumably their traditional arms and tactics were gradually replaced by Roman weaponry and methods (Lazenby 1978: 13). Roman officers called *praefecti sociorum* – apparently three to an *ala* – commanded the allies (Polybios 6.26.5); appointed by the consuls, these prefects probably had a similar role to that of the military tribunes in a legion. At lower levels the *socii* evidently provided their own officers. The **insets** show:

(**1**) Part of a maniple of *triarii*, drawn up as on Plate B.

(**2**) Legionary *centurio* and *signifer*. It is believed that the number of silvered-bronze discs on the *signum* indicated the maniple, counting from the right of the battle line.

(**3**) The six *tribuni* were positioned in front of each legion.

(**4**) The consul, attended by the 12 lictors who were a symbol of his authority.

(**5**) Part of a *turma* of *equites*, with the *decuriones* on the right flank.

5

ala of the right

Legionary
cavalry

3

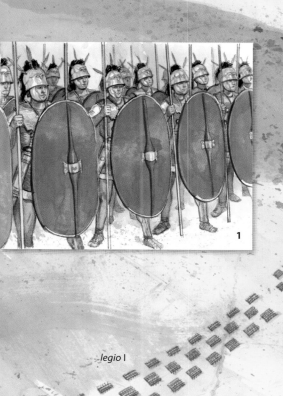

1

Allied
cavalry

ala of the left

legio III

legio I

4

2

provided the phalangites not only with a defensive hedge but also with an unusual bristle of offensive strength. The spearheads of not just the second but also the third, fourth and fifth ranks protruded between the men who formed the front rank, giving 40 per cent more spearheads in the killing zone. To be tactically successful the Macedonian phalanx had to hang together at all costs. With an open field before it, not obstructed by watercourses or tangled with vineyards, the steamroller-like advance of a phalanx, close-packed and bristling with extended *sarissae*, threatened to flatten everything that dared to stand in its way. Lucius Aemilius Paullus, who faced phalangites at Pydna, was left with a lifelong image of terror: 'He considered the formidable appearance of their front, bristling with arms, and was taken with fear and alarm; nothing he had ever seen before was its equal; and much later he frequently used to recall that sight and his own reaction to it.' (Plutarch, *Aemilius Paullus* 19.1)

Hellenistic armies, homogeneous in equipment and training if not in ethnic composition, were in many ways more efficient than the Roman army, but they were also more fragile. Tough, disciplined professionals, serving in units with a clearly defined command structure, were difficult to replace speedily from the limited resources available to each kingdom. These armies also deployed with virtually all their units in a fighting line centred on the deepest possible phalanx, which in Polybios' day was normally 16 ranks deep. As described, the Roman system of deploying in three lines ensured that much of the army was kept out of contact. At both Kynoskephalai and Magnesia the Roman fighting line was broken at one point, but the situation was restored by fresh troops from the reserve lines.

At **Kynoskephalai** (**197** BC), an unidentified tribune in the advancing Roman right wing, becoming aware that things were going worse on the left, used his initiative and peeled off 20 maniples (probably the *principes* and *triarii* of his own unit, *legio II)* to attack the victorious phalanx in the rear. This broke the Macedonian right, and completed the Roman victory. Polybios certainly believed that the flexibility of the legion as opposed to the rigidity of the phalanx was the decisive factor when they met in battle:

Alabaster cinerary urn, 2nd century BC, showing an Etruscan horseman wearing an Etrusco-Corinthian helmet, and a short mail shirt with shoulder doubling and *pteruges*. The staff probably denotes rank, conceivably that of *decurio*. (Volterra, Museo Etrusco, MG278; photo Fields-Carré Collection)

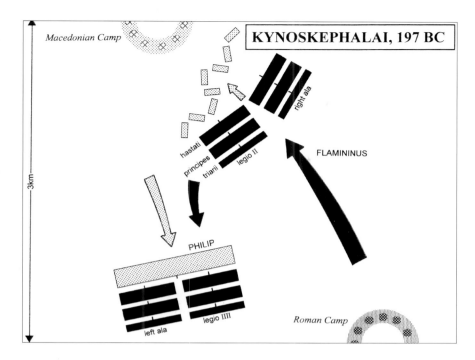

Even in those cases where the phalanx descends to favourable ground, if the whole of it is not used when it can be and the favourable moment is not seized, it is easy to forecast what will happen from the tactics the Romans are now putting into practice. This is not a matter for argument but can easily be proved by past events. The Romans do not attempt to make their line numerically equal to the enemy's, nor do they expose the whole strength of the legions to a frontal attack by the phalanx. Instead they keep part of the forces in reserve while the rest

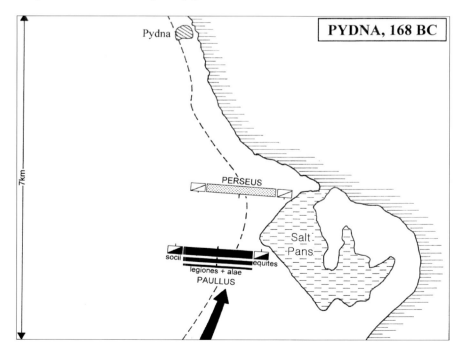

ABOVE LEFT: 3rd-century BC bronze figurine of a warrior wearing a Montefortino helmet but no body armour. He is armed with a sword slung on his right hip, and a *hasta*; the shield is oval, with a wooden spine and metal boss-plate. (Rome, Villa Giulia; photo Sopr. Arch. Etruria Méridionale)

ABOVE RIGHT: Armour was costly, bronze did not rust, and with careful maintenance it might last for generations. This splendid triple-disc cuirass from a tomb at Ksour es-Sad, Tunisia, is complete with the linked-plate straps that passed under the arms and over the shoulders. It was probably taken back to Africa by one of Hannibal's veterans – perhaps one of the Oscan-speaking warriors who fought in the third line at Zama? The decoration of the back plate is identical, showing the same mask of Athena Promachos (i.e. Athena as the 'Foremost Fighter'). A broad bronze belt, the symbol of manhood, would accompany this armour. (Tunis, Musée de Bardo; photo Fields-Carré Collection)

engage the enemy. Later in the battle, whether the phalanx in its charge drives back the troops opposed to it or is driven back by them, in either event it loses its own peculiar formation. For in either pursuing a retreating enemy or falling back before an oncoming one, the phalanx leaves the other units of its own army; at this point the enemy's reserve can occupy the space the phalanx has vacated, and are no longer obliged to attack from the front, but can fall upon it from flank and rear. (18.31.10–32.5)

These comments were made in connection with Philip V's defeat by the Roman army at the Kynoskephalai hills. Seven years later the Roman army crossed over to Asia Minor to confront Philip's fellow Hellenistic prince and rival, Antiochos III, the Seleukid king of Syria, who had assembled a vast army of about 70,000 men. This critical battle, fought on the level plain of **Magnesia (190 BC)**, offers an excellent illustration of the phalanx's inability to manoeuvre effectively. The Romans had about 35,000 troops including 2,800 cavalry. Among their most important allies was Eumenes II of Pergamon who, as ruler of one of the lesser kingdoms of the region, stood to benefit from Antiochos' defeat. His troops were stationed on the right of the Roman line, where the Romans feared they would be outflanked. It was Eumenes' attack that exposed the left flank of the left wing of the phalanx, while it was broken frontally by the Romans. Meantime, the Roman left was being driven from the field by the magnificent Seleukid cavalry commanded by Antiochos himself. Here we have a perfect illustration of the difficulties of the phalanx once its flanks were exposed, as outlined by Polybios above.

An *eques* on the Altar of Domitius Ahenobarbus, dating from perhaps a century after the Volterra urn image. He too wears a mail shirt, but now to thigh length; the downside of the extra protection was the weight – perhaps more than 15kg (*c.* 30lb) – dragging on the shoulders, though a belt could help distribute some of this to the hips. This form of armour spread the impact of a cutting blow efficiently, but a hard thrust with the point might burst through the rings. This rider wears a Boiotian helmet, a style popular with Graeco-Italic horsemen of the period as its wide-spread brim provided unimpaired vision and hearing. Note also the sword slung on the left hip. (Paris, Musée du Louvre, Ma 975; photo Fields-Carré Collection)

Each phalangite sought to maintain his weapon horizontally, poking back and forth to occupy critical empty space should a legionary try to dodge under the 6m-long poles. But if *sarissae* began to waver, or a row of phalangites went down wholesale under a hail of thrown *pila*; if legionaries parrying with *scuta* and jabbing with *gladii* sliced into the interior, or, worse, ripped in from the naked sides of the phalanx – then disaster was immediate. A *sarissa* was only an advantage when the enemy was beyond the sharp end, and the secondary weapon of the trapped phalangite offered him small comfort when faced by the Roman *scutum* and *gladius*.

At Kynoskephalai rough terrain and the flexibility of the legionaries halted Macedonian momentum, and the legions slaughtered 8,000 of Philip's men (Polybios 18.26.12). And at **Pydna (168** BC) Philip's son Perseus had no better luck, as legionaries once again carved deadly gaps in the hitherto steady phalanx – despite its being in double the usual depth – and cut the interior to shreds, butchering more than 20,000 phalangites (Livy 44.42.7). Over almost before it had begun, the engagement at Pydna was considered an exceptionally

Section of frieze decorating the monument to Aemilius Paullus' victory at Pydna, 168 BC – this general was the son of the Lucius Aemilius Paullus killed at Cannae. From left to right: legionary fighting a Macedonian cavalryman, a legionary in a mail shirt, and a *socii* cavalryman also in a mail shirt. It is believed that the frieze depicts the skirmish between opposing watering parties that led to the battle. (Delphi, Archaeological Museum; photo Fields-Carré Collection)

brief affair, yet the Macedonian army – which since the days of Alexander had enjoyed a reputation as the best fighting forces in the Hellenistic world – disappeared forever. 'Battles,' in the sweeping words of Winston Churchill, 'are the punctuation marks of history', and Pydna must qualify as one of his punctuation marks.

SUMMARY

Generals such as Scipio Africanus commanded armies that were 'professional' in their outlook and their operation, but they were not composed of men who might be termed 'regular soldiers'. Roman society had never been broken into the three Indo-European categories – often hereditary – of military, religious, and economic castes, as was common in similar civilizations. Thus throughout our period the soldiers fighting for Rome were its own citizens, for whom the defence of the state was regarded (by the Senate at least) as both a duty and a privilege. Although this was not a regular army, citizens, once enlisted, were subjected to a discipline that was brutal in the extreme, losing most of the legal rights they enjoyed in peacetime until they were discharged. Soldiering was not a career, but a harsh interlude in an almost equally harsh civilian life.

Citizens might well be called upon to serve the Republic on subsequent occasions, but they would not do so with the same comrades, under the same centurions or in the same legions as before. Each legion raised was unique, and would gradually increase in efficiency as it underwent training. Legions that saw active service were often battle-hardened and weapon-trained, but since they were disbanded when the Senate decided they were no longer needed the process would have to begin afresh with new legions. The weakness of the consular system was that few units would have developed a lasting sense of *esprit de corps* or identity. Yet it was with this militia system that the Roman people under arms conquered Italy, defeated their great western rival Carthage, and became the superpower of the Mediterranean world.

The Republic went to war almost annually, and even before the war with Hannibal it normally had the four consular legions (plus the four corresponding *alae*) under arms each year, constituting about one-fifth of the eligible citizens (Hopkins, 1978: 25). Revulsion against war is a relatively modern attitude and we should resist the supposition that the citizens of Rome were generally reluctant to serve. In many societies men from time to

Legionaries on the Altar of Domitius Ahenobarbus, 1st century BC, but wearing gear that had been in use essentially unchanged for perhaps two hundred years. They have crested Montefortino helmets, and ringmail shirts with shoulder doubling for extra protection against downward sword-cuts. The *scutum* shows the characteristic spine and boss; at some 1.2m high by 75cm wide (3ft 10in by 2ft 6in) this shield was large enough to practically hide a legionary, who probably seldom exceeded 1.65m (5ft 5in) tall. To give it an effective mixture of flexibility and resilience it was constructed of three layers of plywood strips glued crosswise and covered in calfskin; to prevent splitting it was bound with iron guttering at the top and bottom. (Paris, Musée du Louvre, Ma 975; photo Fields-Carré Collection)

time have regarded war as a good way of escaping from the grind of day-to-day existence, and as a possible means of getting rich. In the Italian wars many Romans must have fought in the hope of gaining land and booty.

When a man came forward voluntarily, he would presumably be accepted gladly provided he was of suitable age and physical fitness. But there was always a measure of compulsion, and in a loose sense service in the legions of the middle Republic can be likened to 'national service' in many western democracies in the 20th century: an obligation on every fit male to contribute to his country's defence. At first, service in the Roman army entailed a citizen being away from his home – usually a farmstead – for a few weeks or months over the summer. But the need to fight overseas in Iberia, and to leave troops to form permanent garrisons in the newly-won provinces of Sicily and Sardinia, meant that men were away from home for longer periods. This interruption of normal life could easily spell ruin to the soldier-farmers who had traditionally made up the bulk of citizens eligible for conscription. Hopkins (1978: 35) estimates that in 225 BC legionaries comprised 17 per cent of all the adult male citizens, and in 213 BC, at the height of the Second Punic War, no fewer than 29 per cent. Inevitably, what had been seen as a duty and a voluntary obligation took on a somewhat different character.

When the Romans complained to Brennos that he was using dodgy weights to enlarge the agreed ransom, the Gallic chieftain flung his sword into the weighing scale with the stern words 'Vae victis!' – 'woe to the vanquished'. True or not, a more apt riposte cannot be imagined. (Le Brenn et sa part du butin by Paul Joseph Jamin (1893), © musées d'art et d'histoire de La Rochelle, crédits photographiques J+M)

SELECT BIBLIOGRAPHY

Ardent du Picq, C., 1903 (trans Col J. Greely & Maj R. Cotton, 1920). *Battle Studies: Ancient and Modern* (Harrisburg, VA; US Army War College, r/p 1946)

Bath, T., *Hannibal's Campaigns* (Cambridge; Patrick Stephens, 1981)

Carey, B.T., Allfree, J.B. & Cairns, J., *Warfare in the Ancient World.* (Barnsley; Pen & Sword, 2005)

Connolly, P., *Greece and Rome at War,* (Mechanicsburg, PA; Stackpole, 1981, r/p 1998)

Cornell, T.J., *The Beginnings of Rome: Italy and Rome from the Bronze Age to the Punic Wars, c.1000–264 BC* (London; Routledge, 1995)

Cornell, T.J., Rankin, B. & Sabin, P. (eds), *The Second Punic War: A Reappraisal* (London; University of London Press; Bulletin of the Institute of Classical Studies 67, 1996)

David, J-M. (trans. A. Nevill), *The Roman Conquest of Italy* (Oxford; Blackwell)

Dawson, D., *The Origins of Western Warfare* (Boulder, CO; Westview, 1996)

Errington, R.M., *The Dawn of Empire: Rome's Rise to World Power* (London; Hamilton, 1971)

Feugère, M.. (trans D.G. Smith), *Weapons of the Romans* (Stroud; Tempus, 2002)

Fields, N., *The Roman Army of the Punic Wars 264–146 BC* (Oxford, Osprey Battle Orders 27, 2007)

Goldsworthy, A.K., *The Punic Wars* (London; Cassell, 2000)

Harris, W.V., *War and Imperialism in Republican Rome 327–70 BC* (Oxford; Clarendon Press, 1979, r/p 1986)

Head, D., *Armies of the Macedonian and Punic Wars 359 BC–146 BC* (Worthing; Wargames Research Group, 1982)

Hopkins, K., *Conquerors and Slaves* (Cambridge; Cambridge University Press, 1978)

Keppie, L.J.F, *The Making of the Roman Army* (London; Routledge, 1998)

Lazenby, J.F., *Hannibal's War: A Military History of the Second Punic War* (Warminster; Aris & Phillips, 1978)

Lazenby, J.F., *The First Punic War: A Military History* (London; University College Press, 1996)

Miles, G.B., *Livy: Reconstructing Early Rome* (Ithaca, NY; Cornell University Press,1995, r/p 1997)

Nillson, M.P., 'The introduction of hoplite tactics at Rome' in *Journal for Roman Studies* 19 (1929)

Oakley, S.P., 'The Roman conquest of Italy', in J. Rich & G. Shipley (eds), *War and Society in the Roman World* (London; Routledge, 1993)

Parker, H.M.D., *The Roman Legions* (Cambridge; Heffer & Sons, 1928, r/p 1958)

Rawlings, L., 'Condottieri and Clansmen: early Italian raiding, warfare and the state', in K. Hopkins (ed) *Organized Crime in Antiquity* (Cardiff; Classical Press of Wales, 1999, r/p 2009)

Rawson, E., 'The literary sources for the pre-Marian Roman army' in *Papers for the British School at Rome* 39 (1971)

Ross Holloway, R., *The Archaeology of Early Rome and Latium* (London; Routledge, 1994, r/p 1996)

Smith, C.J., *Early Rome and Latium, Economy and Society c.1000–500 BC* (Oxford; Oxford University Press, 1995)

Warry, J., *Warfare in the Classical World* (London; Salamander, 1980)

INDEX